AN UNOFFICIAL

Grand Theft Auto COOKBOOK

Street Eats and Luxe Treats

AN UNOFFICIAL

Grand Theft Auto COOKBOOK

Street Eats and Luxe Treats

Jarrett Melendez

TITAN BOOKS

London

An Insight Editions Book

CONTENTS

THE INTRODUCTION

Welcome to our gastronomic homage to one of the greatest series in the history of gaming. As rabid fans of all things *Grand Theft Auto*, we've sought to combine our expertise in the culinary arts with *GTA*-inspired themes and locations to produce what we consider the ultimate piece of fan fiction—a mouthwatering cookbook devoted to the incomparable *Grand Theft Auto* zeitgeist.

In keeping with that spirit, this book's "menu items" are a bit irreverent, culturally diverse, and subversively appealing. Our epicurean crew dug deep to invent recipes inspired by the fictional food scenes found in Liberty City, Vice City, Los Santos, Las Venturas, and San Fierro—all five major cities of the *GTA* universe. From the haute cuisine of elegant eateries like World of Coq on the Old Venturas Strip, to great grub in backstreet diners like The Greasy Chopper in the bowels of Broker, our highly unofficial recipe list gives you a variety of fantastic dishes for all levels of chefs.

It's not hyperbole to suggest that *Grand Theft Auto* is one of the most popular entities in the history of entertainment, not just videogaming. With more than 440 million units sold and an estimated $9.5 billion in total revenue, the *GTA* series is a juggernaut that very few entertainment franchises can match, especially when it comes to a dedicated fan base. Its massive popularity extends into the modding and fan-fiction communities, with *GTA* lovers creating countless tools and reams of content that expand and pay tribute to the *GTA* universe. This cookbook is our humble attempt to contribute a tasty bit of substance to that ever-growing cosmos.

A BRIEF HISTORY OF GTA

The original *Grand Theft Auto* was developed by DMA Design in Dundee, Scotland, and released in November of 1997. An open-world experience played from a top-down perspective, it established the basic template for *GTA* story development—a low-level criminal climbs in status by completing jobs for local gangs and crime syndicates. The game was set in three cities: Liberty City (based on New York City), San Andreas (then based on San Francisco), and Vice City (based on Miami).

"The game was cops and robbers at first," said Gary Penn, DMA Design's creative director at the time. "[But] nobody wants to be the cop. It's always more fun to be bad." As it turned out, being the bad guy turned into a smashing commercial success; *Grand Theft Auto* sold more than six million units over the first three years after its release.

In 1998, Take-Two Interactive acquired DMA Design's intellectual property, including the rights to *Grand Theft Auto*. Two of the executives brought in to oversee the acquisition were brothers Dan and Sam Houser, who helped co-found a new publishing entity in New York City called Rockstar Games. The DMA Design team produced *Grand Theft Auto 2*, notably bringing in Dan Houser as the game's lead writer. Rather than recreate fictional versions of US cities, GTA 2 was set in a "retrofuturistic metropolis" dubbed Anywhere City, USA. Published by Rockstar, the game hit the shelves in October of 1999 and hit another impressive set of sales milestones.

The next sequel, *Grand Theft Auto III*, is considered a major landmark in videogame history. Set entirely in Liberty City, it was the first truly great open-world experience set in a fully 3D environment. The game's development team featured a core crew of DMA Design working closely with producer Leslie Benzies and a creative team at Rockstar, including writer Dan Houser again. Released in October of 2001, *GTA III* was a spectacular critical and financial success, winning multiple game of the year awards and eventually selling more than 15 million copies.

In March of 2002, DMA Design was renamed Rockstar Studios, and in May, that was changed to Rockstar North—a place that, of course, would go on to become an industry legend. In October of that same year, the first *GTA* title officially developed by Rockstar North was released, *Grand Theft Auto: Vice City*. As the title implies, the game was set in Vice City, the fictional version of Miami. Vice City sold more than 17 million units across all platforms and was named Game of the Year at the annual Golden Joystick Awards.

The franchise took another big leap in 2004 with the release of *Grand Theft Auto: San Andreas*. The story was set in the fictional U.S. state of San Andreas, a California-like region featuring three major cities: Los Santos (based on Los Angeles), San Fierro (San Francisco), and Las Venturas (Las Vegas). Upon its release, fans snapped up 2.1 million copies in just four days, and eventually San Andreas sold more than 27.5 million copies across all platforms—still one of the bestselling games ever.

In 2008, *Grand Theft Auto IV* revisited Liberty City in spectacular fashion, focusing on its glamorous but often brutal urban life and immigrant subcultures. *GTA IV* was another gaming sensation, breaking industry records with more than $500 million sales in the first week of release. The game's protagonist Niko Bellic became a pop culture phenomenon, and like its predecessors, *GTA IV* also won numerous industry accolades including multiple Game of the Year awards.

GTA IV also spawned two episodic expansion packs plus a new handheld title, all set in Liberty City, all released in 2009. The *Grand Theft Auto: The Lost and Damned* expansion featured The Lost MC, a biker gang that first appeared in *GTA IV*; and the *Grand Theft Auto: The Ballad of Gay Tony* expansion focused on the extravagant nightlife of Liberty City's elite at Tony Prince's upscale nightclubs. Finally, *Grand Theft Auto: Chinatown Wars*—released for handheld devices like the Nintendo DS and the PSP—focused on the Liberty City Triads gang.

Four years later, in 2013, Rockstar released one of the most iconic products in entertainment history: *Grand Theft Auto V*, set once again in the fictional state of San Andreas. The vast open-world setting includes the urban sprawl of the City of Los Santos plus the surrounding rural countryside of Blaine County. The game broke all entertainment industry records by earning $1 billion in its first three days of release, and it remains the most profitable entertainment product of all time. *GTA V* also became one of the highest rated games ever on Metacritic, scoring a lofty 97 out of 100 in the site's aggregate of reviews. Its online multiplayer mode, *Grand Theft Auto Online*, attracted millions of users and has generated a formidable digital revenue stream for more than a decade.

LIBERTY CITY

Nobody knows a big city's heart quite like cynical municipal bureaucrats, which explains why Liberty City's official website bills America's greatest metropolis as "the self-proclaimed center of everything." Here, the sun rises and sets hard on the American Dream, every day. Culture, arts, finance, fashion, civic corruption—everything in Liberty City is bigger than life, scattered across its four boroughs.

It all starts in the vertiginous towers of Algonquin, where the well-heeled have perfected the art of rigging the game. To the northeast, rundown, blue-collar Bohan remains a breeding pool for innovative crime-boss candidates. And on the east bank of the Humboldt River, gentrifying Broker shares the big island with mostly middle-class Dukes—an island full of those decent, hardworking folks who comprise the easy marks for the predatory.

Fortunately, when it comes to restaurants, Liberty City's healthy egotism is well justified—along with Paris, Tokyo, and Bangkok, it is undoubtedly one of the great foodie capitals of the world. With a metropolitan area divided into fifty-six distinctive districts, you can find any kind of cuisine and ambience you want. As upscale and Michelin-starred as Algonquin dining can be, we found our favorite dishes for this cookbook in some of Liberty City's less polished neighborhoods, including one in Dukes and four, count 'em, four venues down at the south end of Broker!

STEINWAY BEER GARDEN

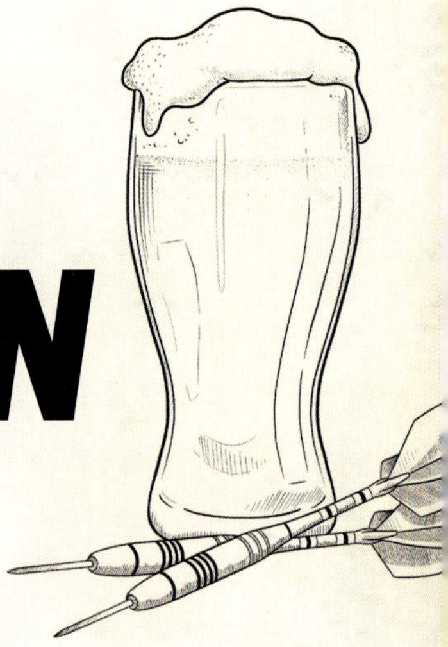

Located at Yorktown Avenue and Morris Street in the Steinway district of Dukes, this famous working-class joint is a classic Irish pub where the favorite activities are drinking, darts, and then considerably more drinking. You won't find a better place to quaff a pint of Blarneys Stout and sample typical Irish pub fare with friends and various armed strangers. (Tip: If you spot any McRearys, you might want to give their family booth a wide berth in passing.) The food here is so comforting that it's served with a lambswool throw from Donegal.

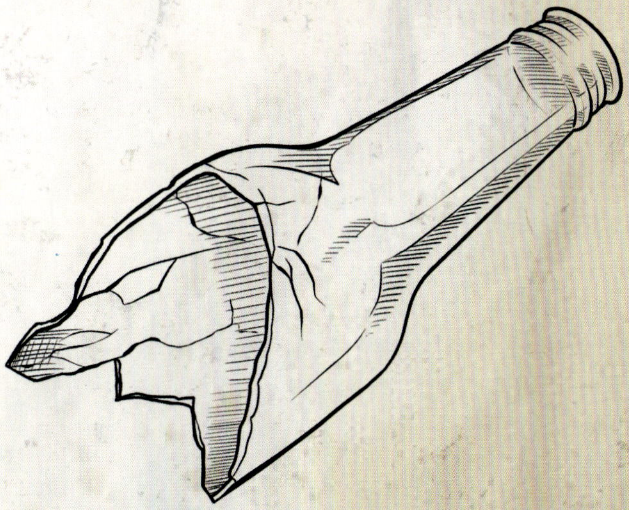

SHEPHERD'S PIE

SERVINGS: 6 to 8 | **COOK TIME:** 75 minutes active, 30 minutes baking | **DIFFICULTY:** Easy | **DIETARY:** N/A

Back in Ireland, this savory pie of minced lamb and vegetables topped with mashed potatoes is as iconic as a shamrock quivering in a County Cork breeze. Transplanted to Liberty City in the Beer Garden, the humble Shepherd's Pie has taken on a whole new role as respite from the grimy street hustle of black-market economics. Tip: Save room for its perfect complement, a slice of Steinway's Chocolate Stout Cake (page 17).

MASHED POTATO TOPPING

4 large russet potatoes, peeled and cut into 2-inch pieces

½ cup half-and-half

6 tablespoons unsalted butter

1½ teaspoons kosher salt

1 teaspoon black pepper

6 ounces sharp, aged cheddar cheese, shredded

LAMB FILLING

2 tablespoons olive oil

1 medium yellow onion, diced

2 large carrots, peeled and diced

2 pounds ground lamb

2 teaspoons kosher salt

½ teaspoon black pepper

4 tablespoons tomato paste

3 cloves garlic, minced

1 teaspoon fresh thyme leaves

½ teaspoon fresh minced rosemary leaves

2 tablespoons unsalted butter

1 tablespoon all-purpose flour

1 cup low-sodium chicken stock

1 cup frozen peas

1 cup frozen corn

1. Prepare the mashed potato topping. Bring a large pot of water to a boil. Add the potatoes and cook until a sharp knife easily pierces them, 15 to 20 minutes. Drain in a colander. Return the pot to the stove and place on medium-low heat. Add the half-and-half and butter and heat until melted. Process the potatoes through a ricer or food mill back into the pot (if you don't have one, just return them to the pot and mash with a potato masher). Season with salt and pepper, taste, and add more salt or pepper to your liking. Stir in three-quarters of the shredded cheese.
2. Heat the oven to 375°F. While the oven heats, prepare the lamb filling. In a large skillet or Dutch oven, heat the oil over medium-high heat until shimmering. Add the onion and carrots and cook, stirring occasionally, until the onions are softened and turning translucent and the carrots are just barely tender, 8 to 12 minutes.
3. Add the ground lamb, season with salt and pepper, and cook, breaking the lamb up into small bits with a wooden spoon until the lamb is just cooked through, 5 to 8 minutes. Stir in the tomato paste, garlic, thyme, rosemary, butter, and flour. Reduce the heat to medium and cook, stirring constantly, until the tomato paste darkens to a brick-red color and the mixture loses its raw-flour smell, 3 to 5 minutes.
4. Stir in the chicken stock, peas, and corn. Increase the heat back to medium-high and cook, stirring constantly, until the sauce thickens and reduces slightly, 4 to 7 minutes. Season to taste with additional salt and pepper if needed and remove from the heat.
5. Tip the lamb filling into a large casserole (a 9-by-13-inch baking dish will work well), and top with dollops of the mashed potatoes. Smooth the mashed potatoes into a single layer and top with the reserved cheese.
6. Bake the shepherd's pie for 25 to 30 minutes, until the filling is bubbling and the potatoes are golden brown on top. Let sit for 10 minutes before serving. Leftover shepherd's pie can be stored in the casserole, tightly covered, in the fridge for up to 5 days.

STEINWAY'S CHOCOLATE STOUT CAKE

SERVINGS: 10 to 12 | **COOK TIME:** 20 minutes active, 40 minutes baking | **DIFFICULTY:** Intermediate | **DIETARY:** Vegetarian

A Minnesota company named Nordic Ware invented a ring-shaped cake pan in the 1950s and gave it a German name. Little did they know that seventy-five years later some innovative Irish chef in Liberty City would appropriate their creation to craft a truly brilliant concept: Guinness in a Bundt! Imagine a perfect ring of luscious chocolate Bundt cake infused with a legendary Irish stout and topped with an Irish cream glaze. Not even a corrupt papal conclave would forgive such a sinful indulgence!

8 tablespoons unsalted butter, plus more for greasing

1 pint Irish stout beer

¾ cup cocoa powder

½ teaspoon instant coffee granules

2½ cups all-purpose flour

2½ teaspoons baking soda

1 teaspoon kosher salt

3 large eggs

1 cup dark brown sugar

¾ cup granulated sugar

1 tablespoon vanilla extract

1 cup buttermilk, plus more as needed

IRISH CREAM ICING

1½ cups powdered sugar, sifted

3 to 4 tablespoons Irish cream liqueur

1 teaspoon vanilla extract

1. Preheat the oven to 350°F. Grease a large Bundt pan with butter.
2. Pour the beer into a large saucepan. Bring to a simmer over medium heat, stirring occasionally. Keep an eye on it, as it will bubble quite a bit as the carbonation gets cooked out. Keep simmering until reduced by about half, about 10 minutes. You should end up with 1 cup—if you end up with less, just make up the difference with a bit of extra buttermilk later on.
3. Reduce the heat to low and add the butter, cooking just until melted, stirring occasionally. Remove from the heat and stir in the cocoa powder and coffee granules. Transfer to a large bowl and set aside to cool.
4. While the cocoa mixture cools, sift together the flour, baking soda, and salt into a small bowl. Set aside.
5. Beat the eggs, one at a time, into the cocoa mixture until smooth. Add the brown sugar, granulated sugar, and vanilla, beating until smooth. Stir in one-third of the flour mixture, mixing until just incorporated. Add half the buttermilk, stirring until smooth. Repeat with the remaining flour and buttermilk. (Note: If you ended up with less than 1 cup of reduced beer, make up that amount with buttermilk in this step—if you ended up with ¾ cup of beer, add ¼ cup of buttermilk to this step, for example.)
6. Pour the cake batter into the prepared Bundt pan, smoothing into an even layer. Give the pan a couple of sharp taps on the counter to knock out any large air bubbles. Bake for 30 to 40 minutes, until a toothpick inserted in the center of the cake comes out mostly clean with a few moist crumbs clinging to it.
7. Place the Bundt pan on a wire cooling rack and let the cake cool completely. Place a plate over the top of the cake and invert it—it should fall out of the pan on its own. Otherwise, give the cake pan a sharp, downward shake and let gravity do its thing.
8. Add the powdered sugar, 3 tablespoons of Irish cream, and vanilla extract to a medium bowl. Beat on low with an electric handheld mixer until moistened, then increase the speed to medium and beat until smooth and pourable, but still thick. It should move slowly, sort of like lava. If it's too thick, add a bit more Irish cream, 1 teaspoon at a time and up to 1 tablespoon, stirring between additions and checking the consistency.
9. Pour the icing over the top of the cake, gently spreading it so it slowly drips down the sides of the cake. Let sit at room temperature until the icing sets, 20 to 30 minutes, before slicing and serving. Keep leftover cake covered at room temperature for up to 3 days.

IRISH HOT COFFEE

SERVINGS: 2 | **COOK TIME:** 10 minutes | **DIFFICULTY:** Easy | **DIETARY:** Vegetarian, Gluten free

Nothing lifts a young lad's spirits quite like hot coffee, sensual and steaming. Same goes for the lasses and everyone between and beyond. Let's face it . . . a little hot coffee is always the best way to start and end your day. But the Beer Garden elevates this everyman beverage to entirely new heights with a wickedly stimulating Irish concoction. Just add a bit of Irish whiskey and a squirt of Irish cream into your goblet for a truly carnal touch. (Note: Don't tell anyone, but the secret to Steinway's hot coffee is in the grinding. The harder you grind, the more satisfying the entire experience.)

IRISH CREAM WHIPPED CREAM

½ cup heavy cream

2 tablespoons Irish cream liqueur

1 tablespoon powdered sugar

TO ASSEMBLE

2 cups hot coffee

2 tablespoons dark brown sugar

2 ounces Irish whiskey

1 ounce Irish cream liqueur

1. In a medium bowl with a handheld mixer on medium-high, beat together the heavy cream, Irish cream liqueur, and powdered sugar until soft peaks form. Chill until ready to use.
2. In a spouted, heatproof measuring cup, whisk together the coffee, brown sugar, whiskey, and Irish cream until the sugar dissolves. Divide between two 12-ounce clear coffee mugs, then top with the whipped cream. Serve immediately.

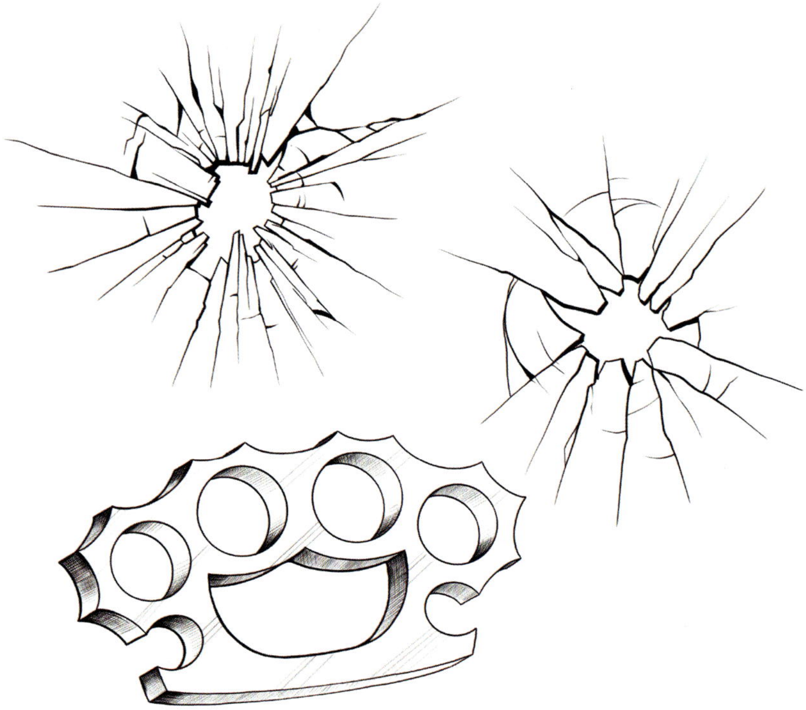

COMRADES BAR

Located on Mohawk Avenue in the diverse Broker neighborhood of Hove Beach, this tough tavern is popular with local Russian immigrants and gangs. Founded by the late, great Vlad Glebov, Comrades persists even in times of uncertainty and peril. One reason might be the mouthwatering shashlik and beloved blini, so special to local patrons. Another might be the backroom money laundering operation. Whatever the case, be sure to say hey to longtime mixologist Mickey behind the bar . . . and we recommend maintaining easy access to that shiv strapped to your ankle.

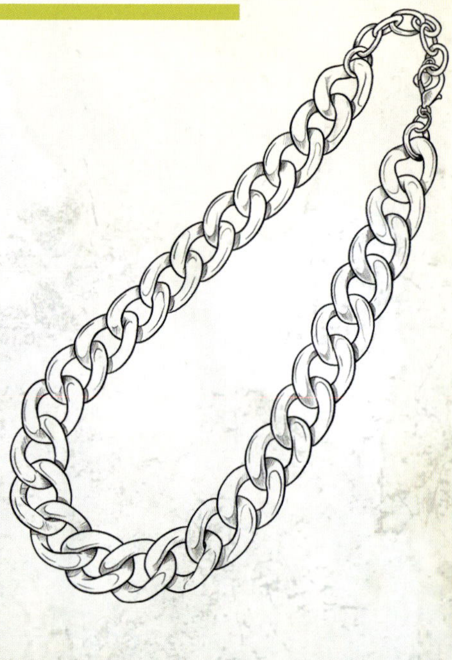

BLINI WITH SMOKED SALMON

SERVINGS: 4 to 6 | **COOK TIME:** 30 minutes | **DIFFICULTY:** Easy | **DIETARY:** N/A

Blini is another one of those old-school Slavic dishes that, over time, has transcended its regional roots to become a global gastronomic sensation. These savory, crepe-like, bite-size pancakes, served with a variety of toppings, can be a work of culinary art. The Comrades Bar rendering features crème fraîche, smoked salmon, and a frond of fresh dill. As for the elephant in the room: yes, blini is a bratva favorite. But if the Russian mob loves something this much, it just might be in your best interest to try it because you'll probably love it too (if you know what's good for you, my friend).

¼ cup all-purpose flour

¼ cup buckwheat flour

1 tablespoon granulated sugar

½ teaspoon kosher salt

¼ teaspoon baking soda

⅓ cup whole milk

2 large eggs, separated

3 tablespoons unsalted butter, melted and cooled, plus more for pan or griddle

TO ASSEMBLE

Crème fraîche

Smoked salmon

Fresh dill

1. In a small bowl, whisk together the flours, sugar, salt, and baking soda. In a separate medium bowl, beat together the milk, egg yolks, and butter until smooth. Stir in the flour mixture until combined.
2. In another medium bowl or in the bowl of a stand mixer, beat the egg whites on medium-high speed (using a handheld electric mixer if not using a stand mixer) to soft peaks. Carefully fold the beaten egg whites into the mixture from step 1.
3. In a nonstick skillet or on a griddle, heat 1 tablespoon of butter over medium heat, spreading the butter in a thin layer across the entire cooking surface. Use a 1-tablespoon measuring spoon to drop the batter into the skillet. How many you can cook at a time will depend on the size of your skillet or griddle—use your best judgment here and give yourself space to be able to comfortably flip the blini. Cook until bubbles form on the surface of each blini and the bottoms are golden brown, 2 to 3 minutes.
4. Flip the blini and cook for 1 to 2 minutes, until cooked through. Transfer to a wire rack to cool, then repeat the process with the remaining blini batter. If the pan looks dry, add another tablespoon of butter as needed.
5. While the blini cool, prepare the toppings. Stir the crème fraîche until smooth, then cut the smoked salmon into roughly 1-inch pieces. Roll each piece of salmon into a cone shape. Pull small fronds of dill from the bunch, about ½ inch long. For the salmon and dill, cut and pull as many pieces as you need to top each blini.
6. Top each blini with a small dollop of crème fraîche, about a ½ teaspoon per blini. Gently place a cone of salmon on top of the crème fraîche, pressing lightly to secure it. Top the salmon with a piece of dill. Serve immediately.

SHASHLIK

SERVINGS: 4 | **COOK TIME:** 4 hours marinating, 20 minutes active | **DIFFICULTY:** Easy | **DIETARY:** Gluten free

No Russian of sane mind can resist the smell of seasoned meat sizzling on a grill. Whatever else the motherland has produced of value—and we're not here to debate that list—nothing surpasses the cultural greatness of shashlik, particularly the incarnation that comes out of the Comrades kitchen. Passed down through generations of starving peasants, these succulent skewers of marinated lamb and red bell peppers migrated from rural Russia into Moscow and St. Petersburg in the early twentieth century . . . and soon became one of Eastern Europe's most popular and pervasive street foods.

1 tablespoon lemon juice

1 teaspoon lemon zest

2 tablespoons olive oil, plus more for greasing

1 teaspoon fresh oregano, finely chopped

1 teaspoon fresh thyme, finely chopped

1 teaspoon kosher salt

½ teaspoon black pepper

1 pound lamb loin, cut into 1-inch cubes

2 red bell peppers, cut into 1-inch pieces

1. In a small bowl or sealable plastic or glass container, whisk to combine the lemon juice, lemon zest, olive oil, oregano, thyme, salt, and pepper. Add the cubes of lamb, toss to combine, and then cover the bowl. Keep refrigerated for 4 hours, tossing once halfway through.
2. If using bamboo skewers, soak them in water for at least 30 minutes before threading the meat and peppers.
3. Divide the marinated meat and bell peppers among the skewers, alternating between pieces of meat and bell pepper as you work. Set aside while you heat the grill or broiler.
4. **If using a charcoal grill:** Fill a chimney starter with charcoal, then pack the bottom with newspaper or crumpled brown paper bags. Light the starter and wait for the coals to light all the way through. The coals are ready to use once they are glowing and coated in ash. While the coals light, brush a thin layer of neutral oil on the grill grate (or spray with cooking spray meant for use with a grill). Dump the coals in an even layer on the bottom of your grill. Place the grill grate over the coals, cover the grill, and allow to preheat for about 5 minutes. **If using a gas grill:** Oil the grates, light the burners on high, and allow the grill to preheat for about 5 minutes. **If using a broiler:** Place an oven rack directly under the broiler.
5. **If using a grill:** Place the skewers over the hottest part of the grill and cook until well seared with some light charring on the meat and peppers, 2 to 3 minutes. Flip, and cook for 2 to 3 minutes longer. Transfer to a serving platter and let rest in a warm place for 5 to 10 minutes before serving. **If using a broiler:** Place the skewers on a baking sheet and put it directly under the broiler. Cook until well seared and lightly charred on top, 2 to 5 minutes (the actual timing will depend on the strength of your broiler—start checking the skewers periodically after the first 2 minutes). Flip the skewers and cook for another 2 to 5 minutes. Remove the pan from the broiler and let the skewers rest in a warm place for 5 to 10 minutes before serving.

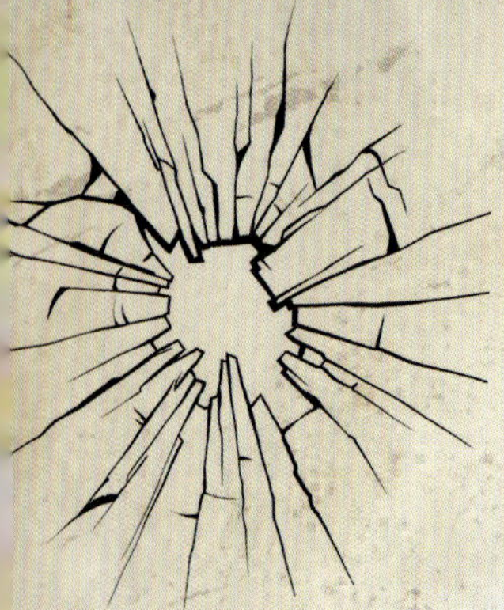

PERESTROIKA

You can't miss Perestroika's flashy awning over the front entrance on Tulsa Street in Hove Beach, Broker. This old-school Russian cabaret was once famous for sawing women in half—an illusionist magic trick, or so we assume. These days, the place has become a Russian Mafia hangout, featuring a bar and a stage where remarkably strange acts still perform as if they just crept out of a Baltic fog. But don't let the club's unsettling theatricality fool you—Perestroika's dining area serves some of the finest Russian foods since the breakup of the Soviet Union. Just don't crack any Sputnik jokes; Chef Yevgeny will take it personally.

PAPA'S PIROZHKI

SERVINGS: Makes 12 | **COOK TIME:** 1 hour active, 3 hours rising, 25 minutes baking | **DIFFICULTY:** Hard | **DIETARY:** Vegetarian

This classic Eastern European comfort food is another one of those legendary folk dishes that trundled like an oxcart through the Russian countryside for many, many generations. Then one day, boom! You walk into Perestroika and it hits your modern, gentrified taste buds like a hypersonic missile launched from the Transcaucasus. The chef starts with ovals of yeast-leavened dough, ladled thick with tasty fillings—cabbage, onions, and farmer cheese are traditional starters, plus (in this version) a dollop of dill-seasoned ground beef. Then you pinch them shut and pop the boat-shaped buns into the oven, baking to golden-brown perfection.

DOUGH

¾ cup whole milk, lukewarm

2 teaspoons sugar, divided

2 teaspoons active dry yeast

2½ cups all-purpose flour

1 teaspoon kosher salt

1 large egg, lightly beaten

4 tablespoons unsalted butter, softened

Olive oil, for greasing the bowl

FILLING

2 tablespoons olive oil

1 pound ground beef

2½ teaspoons kosher salt, divided, plus more as needed

1 teaspoon black pepper, divided, plus more as needed

1 small onion, diced

2 cups finely chopped green cabbage

½ cup farmer cheese

¼ cup finely chopped fresh dill

1 large egg

1 tablespoon water

1. In a small bowl, whisk together the milk, 1 teaspoon of sugar, and the yeast. Let sit for 5 minutes until foamy.
2. Meanwhile, in the bowl of a stand mixer fitted with the dough hook attachment, combine the remaining 1 teaspoon of sugar, the flour, and salt. Mix on low to combine. Add the milk mixture and the egg and mix until a shaggy dough forms. Increase the speed of the mixer to medium and continue mixing until the dough is smooth, about 5 minutes longer. Add half the butter and mix until it has completely incorporated, then add the remaining butter, mixing until fully incorporated.
3. Continue mixing until the dough is smooth and elastic, 15 minutes longer. It should pass the windowpane test (this is when you pull a small piece of dough from the main mass and gently stretch it between your fingers. If it stretches thin enough to become almost transparent without tearing, the dough passes the test. If it doesn't, keep mixing for a few minutes at a time until it does). Add the dough to a lightly oiled bowl, cover, and let rest for 1 to 2 hours, until puffed and doubled in volume.
4. While the dough mixes and rises, prepare the filling. In a large Dutch oven, heat the oil oven over medium-high heat until shimmering. Add the ground beef, season with 1 teaspoon of salt and ½ teaspoon of black pepper, and cook while breaking apart with a wooden spoon. Cook, stirring occasionally, until well browned and cooked through, 7 to 10 minutes.
5. Transfer the beef to a large bowl with a slotted spoon. Drain the excess fat from the Dutch oven, leaving about 2 tablespoons behind to cook the vegetables. Return the Dutch oven to the stove, still over medium-high heat, and add the onions. Cook, stirring occasionally, until softened, about 5 minutes.

CONTINUED ON NEXT PAGE

PAPA'S PIROZHKI (CONTINUED)

6. Add the cabbage to the pot, season with the remaining 1½ teaspoons of salt and ½ teaspoon of pepper, and cook, stirring occasionally, until tender, 7 to 10 minutes. Transfer the cabbage and onions to the bowl of beef and toss to combine. Cover and chill in the fridge until the dough is ready. The filling can be prepared up to this point up to 3 days in advance—just keep it in a sealed container in the fridge until you're ready to make the pirozhki.
7. Finish making the filling by stirring in the farmer cheese and dill. Season to taste with additional salt and pepper as needed. Keep chilled until ready to use. Line two half-sheet pans with parchment.
8. Turn the dough out onto a lightly floured surface and gently punch down the dough to remove excess air. Divide into 12 equal pieces. Keep the dough portions in a sealed container so they don't dry out as you work.
9. Roll each piece of dough out into a rough oval shape about 6 inches by 3 inches, and ¼ inch thick. Fill with about ¼ cup of filling, then stretch the dough edges up around the filling, pinching to seal. Place seam-side down on one of the prepared pans. Gently shape into a boat-like shape. Cover with plastic wrap. Repeat the process with the remaining dough and filling, placing six pirozhki on each pan. Let rise in a warm place for 1 hour, or until well puffed.
10. While the pirozhki rest, preheat the oven to 350°F. Once the pirozhki are ready to bake, beat the egg and water. Brush the pirozhki with a thin layer of the egg mixture, then bake until golden brown, 20 to 25 minutes, rotating the pans about halfway through the baking time. Transfer the pirozhki to a wire cooling rack to cool. Serve warm or at room temperature. Once the pirozhki have cooled, keep in a sealed container in the fridge for up to 3 days. To reheat, bake in a 350°F oven for about 10 minutes or until warmed through.

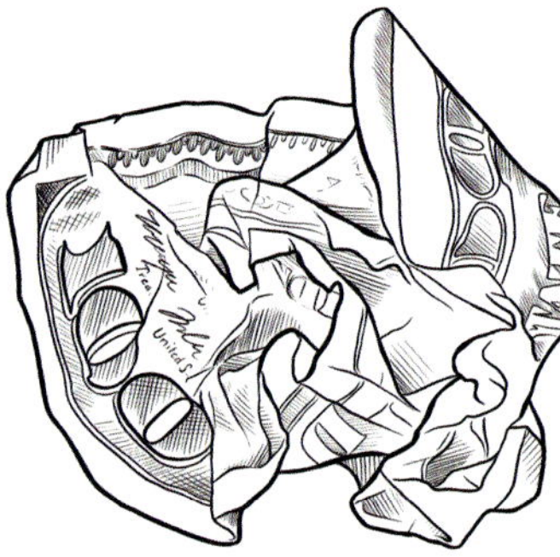

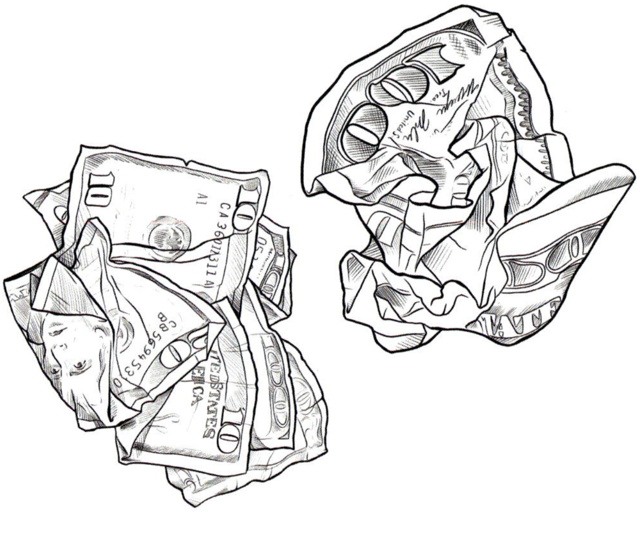

PB 96888592 H
SERIES 2017 A

RUSSIAN SALAD

SERVINGS: 6 to 8 | **COOK TIME:** 1 hour active, 4 hours chilling | **DIFFICULTY:** Easy | **DIETARY:** Vegetarian, Gluten free

Welcome to Perestroika! Let's play our Russian rendition of "Don't ask, just eat." First, toss down a chilled 50-milligram shot of Cherenkov Premium Vodka. (Tip: Save the rest for your next Molotov cocktail.) Then stab your fork into a bowl of our iconic post-Soviet mystery medley. What do you taste? So many things! Boiled potatoes, carrots, peas, eggs, cornichons (those tart, tiny pickles). Vinegar (or maybe pickle brine), dill, mayonnaise. Creamy, tangy, filling. Invented in the 1860s by Lucien Olivier, legendary chef of the Hermitage, Moscow's most celebrated eatery, the Russian Salad was so wildly popular it became a signature dish of the Tsarist Empire. Now it's the toast of Liberty City.

4 large eggs

2 large waxy potatoes (red or yellow), peeled and cut into 1-inch cubes

4 medium carrots, peeled and cut into ½-inch-thick coins

1 cup frozen peas

½ cup cornichons, drained and diced

1 tablespoon white wine vinegar, apple cider vinegar, or pickle brine

½ to ¾ cup mayonnaise

½ teaspoon kosher salt, plus more as needed

½ teaspoon black pepper, plus more as needed

2 tablespoons finely chopped fresh dill

1. Pour about 1 inch of water into a medium saucepan. Place a steamer basket in the saucepan, then bring the water to a boil over high heat. Add the eggs to the steamer basket and steam for 12 minutes. While they steam, fill a large bowl with ice water. Once the eggs have finished steaming, transfer them to the ice water and let them cool for 20 minutes.
2. While the eggs chill, bring a large pot of salted water to a boil. Add the potatoes and carrots. Bring back to a boil, then reduce to a simmer and cook, uncovered, for 15 to 20 minutes, until the potatoes and carrots are tender enough to be easily pierced with a skewer or paring knife (but not so tender that they completely fall apart). Strain through a colander and run cold water over them to stop them from cooking. Set aside to continue draining and cooling.
3. Bring a small pot of water to a boil over high heat. Add the frozen peas, return to a boil, and cook until tender, but still bright green, 2 to 3 minutes. Drain and cool under cold running water.
4. Once the eggs are done cooling, crack them all over and remove the shells under running water. Dice them, then add them to a large bowl, along with the potatoes, carrots, peas, and cornichons.
5. In a small bowl, whisk the mayonnaise, vinegar or pickle brine, salt, pepper, and dill together until smooth. Pour over the mixture from step 4 and gently stir together with a rubber spatula, taking care not to break up the potatoes and carrots. Taste and adjust the seasoning as needed with additional salt and pepper. Cover the bowl and chill for at least 4 hours or overnight before serving. Keep leftovers stored in a sealed container in the fridge for up to 4 days.

APPLE SHARLOTKA

SERVINGS: 8 to 12 | **COOK TIME:** 20 minutes active, 1 hour baking | **DIFFICULTY:** Intermediate | **DIETARY:** Vegetarian

First made to honor Empress Elizabeth, the wife of Tsar Alexander I, this once-elaborate royal dessert eventually evolved into the simpler, more rustic iteration it is today. The real key to this classic Russian apple cake is, no surprise, the apples. You want medium tart, if possible—Granny Smith usually works best. These work in tandem with the sugar, vanilla, ground cinnamon, and final dusting of powdered sugar to create a concoction so deliciously contradictory, even ex-KGB goons are confused by it.

1 cup all-purpose flour

1 teaspoon ground cinnamon

¼ teaspoon ground nutmeg

4 medium tart apples, such as Granny Smith, peeled, cored, and cut into ¼-inch slices

1¼ cups granulated sugar, divided

1 tablespoon lemon juice

4 large eggs

½ teaspoon kosher salt

2 teaspoons vanilla extract

1 tablespoon powdered sugar

1. Preheat the oven to 350°F. Grease and line an 8-inch springform cake with a circle of parchment.
2. In a small bowl, whisk together the flour, cinnamon, and nutmeg. Set aside.
3. In a medium bowl, toss together the apples, ¼ cup of granulated sugar, and the lemon juice. Set aside.
4. In a large bowl, beat the eggs with a handheld electric mixer on medium speed until foamy (you can also use a stand mixer fitted with the whisk attachment). Add the salt and vanilla, then continue beating, increasing the speed to medium-high. Gradually add the remaining 1 cup of granulated sugar and continue beating until the mixture is very pale, light, fluffy, and ribbony (as in, the beaters leave a ribbony looking trail behind them that take a few seconds to melt back into the mixture).
5. Fold the flour mixture into the egg mixture in two additions, folding just until the flour mixture is fully incorporated both times. Scoop about one-quarter of this mixture into the bottom of the cake pan, spreading it into an even layer.
6. Add the apples and any accumulated juices to the cake pan, then top with the remaining cake batter. Give the pan a couple of quick sharp taps to knock out any big air bubbles and to help the cake batter seep in around the apple slices. Bake for 50 to 60 minutes, until a toothpick inserted into the center of the cake comes out clean (just be careful not to poke too far or you'll hit the apples and the toothpick may come out looking wet).
7. Set the cake pan on a wire cooling rack to cool completely. Run a thin knife around the edge of the cake, then remove the outer ring of the springform pan. Transfer to a serving platter and dust with powdered sugar. Keep the cake tightly wrapped at room temperature for up to 2 days or in the fridge for up to 5 days.

69th STREET

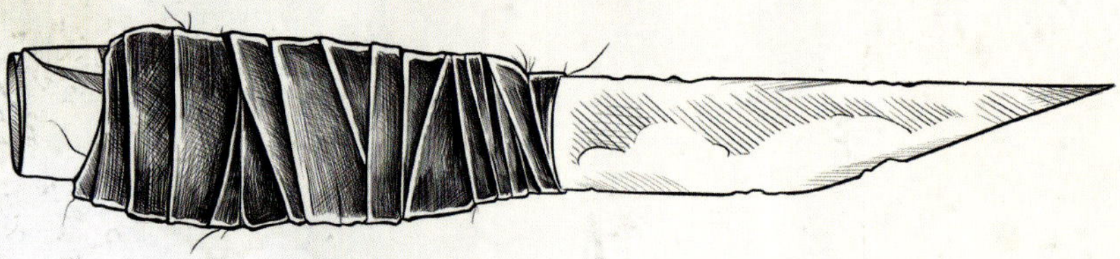

Whenever you're in Hove Beach, head directly to the intersection of Mohawk Avenue and Bart Street, southwest corner, to sample the classic diner fare to be found at this casual Critics' Choice restaurant. Bring your partner here for the vintage 1950s ambience featuring a railcar-inspired streamliner design, retro-shabby decor, and its famous sixty-nine-cent specials—a burger with one bun on top, another inverted on the bottom. As its website so succinctly puts it: Who could resist such greasy allure?

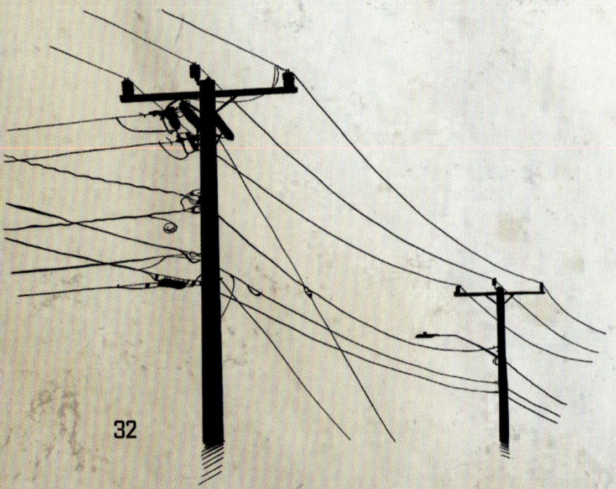

ALGONQUIN COCKTAIL

SERVINGS: 1 cocktail | **COOK TIME:** 2 minutes | **DIFFICULTY:** Easy | **DIETARY:** Vegan, Gluten free

Sometimes a classic is just a classic, no explanation given or required. Named after Liberty City's most famous and distinctive borough, this drink is the perfect blend of straight-up business, high-class pleasure, and smooth-talking con. Bourbon, sweet vermouth, a dash of bitters, a cherry—simple but stylish, slick yet formidable. A drink for hustlers, high rollers, and the ones who own the skyline. Like we said, a classic.

2 ounces rye whiskey

½ ounce sweet vermouth

½ ounce amaro

2 dashes orange bitters

2 dashes cherry bitters

1 cocktail cherry

2-inch piece orange peel

1. In a cocktail mixing glass filled with ice, add the whiskey, vermouth, and amaro. Add the orange and cherry bitters. Stir vigorously with a cocktail spoon for 15 to 30 seconds.
2. Strain into a chilled cocktail glass. Drop the cherry into the glass, twist the piece of orange peel over the top of the glass and around the rim, then stick the orange peel into the glass so it stands upright leaning against the rim of the glass. Serve immediately.

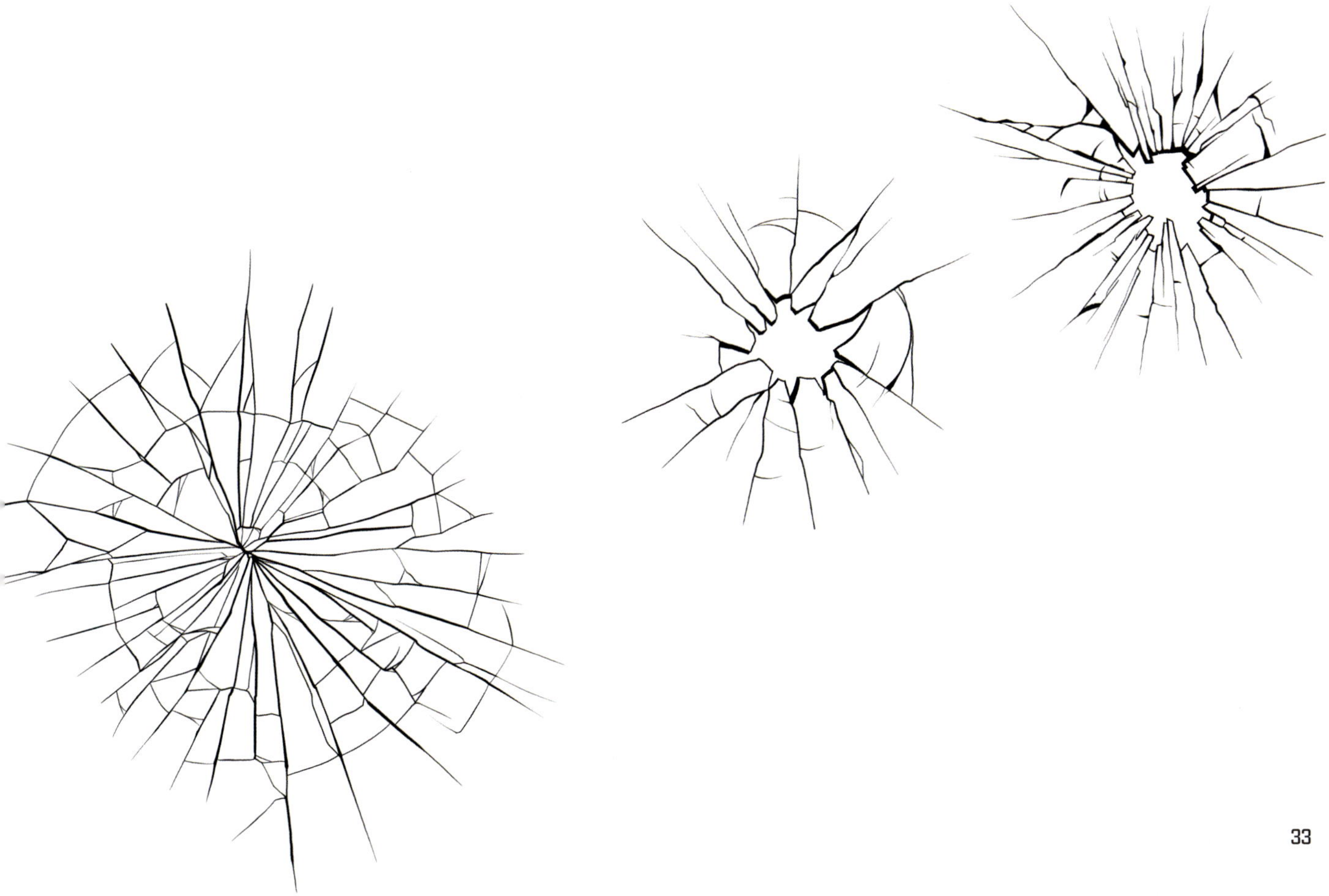

BART'S BAGEL & LOX

SERVINGS: 4 | **COOK TIME:** 15 minutes | **DIFFICULTY:** Easy | **DIETARY:** N/A

No Liberty City diner worth its salt would neglect this essential food item. In the late nineteenth century, hardy Polish immigrants brought a curious circular bread called the "bagel" to Liberty City, and it immediately became a mainstay of urban life. Soon after, Scandinavian newcomers—whose fishermen had perfected the art of preserving their catch in brine—introduced the delicacy of "lox" (brined salmon) to the city. Some genius decided to combine them, adding cream cheese, capers, tomato, and cucumber to conjure a cult classic, beloved from the pricey high-rises of Middle Park West to the crime-ridden backstreets of Chase Point. Indeed, Bart's iconic version with a zesty schmear has fueled so much "financial activity" in Liberty City, it might as well be listed as a brokerage firm.

1 large tomato, thinly sliced

Kosher salt

Black pepper

8 ounces cream cheese, softened

2 teaspoons fresh dill, finely chopped

1 teaspoon lemon juice

½ teaspoon lemon zest

4 bagels (see note)

8 ounces smoked salmon

2 teaspoons capers, drained and rinsed

1. Lay the tomato slices out on a cutting board. Season gently with salt and pepper. Let sit while you prepare the remaining ingredients.
2. In a small bowl, stir to combine the cream cheese, dill, lemon juice, and lemon zest until smooth and creamy. Lemon-dill cream cheese can be prepared up to 3 days in advance.
3. Split and toast the bagels to your desired brownness. Divide the cream cheese evenly between all eight bagel halves.
4. Dab the tomato slices with a paper towel to soak up any excess tomato juice. Lay one slice of tomato on each of the bottom halves of the bagels.
5. Divide the smoked salmon evenly among the bagels, topping the tomato slices with the salmon.
6. Scatter ½ teaspoon of capers on each of the top bagel halves, gently pressing them into the cream cheese to keep them secure. Place the bagel tops on the bottoms, then slice each bagel sandwich crosswise before serving.

NOTE: Choose your favorite bagels, preferably fresh from a bakery! Plain, sesame, poppy, everything—they're all great options.

THE GREASY CHOPPER

There's no better place to hawk heroin and fence blood diamonds than this gritty and often harrowing biker's dive. Located down in the bowels of Broker, the Greasy Chopper is the only place a self-respecting MC leader like Johnny Klebitz would bring his Lost boys from Alderney to binge and brawl. The Chopper's Firefly Island location is also a great slumming spot for upscale customers seeking surprisingly great eats and the exhilaration of an authentic near-death experience.

LIBERTY CITY MC CHILI

SERVINGS: 4 to 6 | **COOK TIME:** 90 minutes | **DIFFICULTY:** Easy | **DIETARY:** Gluten free

Quick and easy, like a gas stop on the open road. This spicy recipe is a perfect prelude to long rides and brutal membership purges. You may find similar ingredients listed in other chili recipes, but you won't find a better "cook" anywhere from Alderney to Blaine County, San Andreas. The Chopper's gritty little secret: a patented Dutch oven technique. Its browning and slow-cook capacity gives Liberty City MC Chili a hearty, robust piquancy with a kick—a kick that, if truth be told, brings more badass bikers to the Greasy Chopper than to the annual Sturgis Motorcycle Rally.

2 tablespoons neutral oil

1 pound ground beef

2 teaspoons kosher salt, divided, plus more as needed

1 large onion, diced

3 cloves garlic, minced

1 tablespoon ancho chile powder

1 tablespoon ground cumin

2 teaspoons sweet paprika

2 teaspoons ground coriander

1 teaspoon chipotle powder

1 teaspoon black pepper, plus more as needed

1 teaspoon garlic powder

1 teaspoon onion powder

1 teaspoon hot smoked paprika

1 teaspoon dried Mexican oregano or marjoram

1 cup beef stock

2 tablespoons stone-ground mustard

One 28-ounce can whole plum tomatoes

One 14-ounce can fire-roasted diced tomatoes

One 14-ounce can kidney beans, drained and rinsed

One 14-ounce can cannellini beans, drained and rinsed

1 teaspoon instant coffee granules

1 tablespoon Worcestershire sauce

TO SERVE

Sour cream

Shredded cheddar and jack cheeses

1. In a large Dutch oven, heat the oil over medium-high heat until shimmering. Add the beef and break it up into small chunks with a wooden spoon. Season with 1 teaspoon of kosher salt. Cook, stirring occasionally, until well browned and cooked through. Use a slotted spoon to transfer the cooked beef to a clean plate.
2. Add the onions to the Dutch oven and cook, stirring occasionally, until softened and beginning to turn brown at the edges, 7 to 10 minutes. Add the garlic, chile powder, cumin, sweet paprika, coriander, chipotle powder, black pepper, garlic powder, onion powder, smoked paprika, Mexican oregano, and remaining 1 teaspoon of kosher salt. Cook, stirring constantly, until fragrant, about 1 minute.
3. Return the cooked beef to the Dutch oven, along with the beef stock , mustard, and whole tomatoes. Mash the tomatoes with a potato masher or wooden spoon, then add the diced tomatoes. Bring to a boil, then reduce to a simmer.
4. Cover the Dutch oven with the lid slightly ajar and cook, stirring occasionally, for 30 to 45 minutes, until the beef is tender. Add the kidney and cannellini beans, coffee granules, and Worcestershire sauce, cover, and simmer for another 15 minutes, stirring occasionally. Season to taste with additional salt and pepper as desired. Serve the chili with sour cream and shredded cheese. Keep leftover chili in a sealed container in the fridge for up to 5 days.

BIKER BREAKFAST BURRITO

SERVINGS: 4 | **COOK TIME:** 45 minutes | **DIFFICULTY:** Easy | **DIETARY:** N/A

When your MC has a consequential brawl looming ahead, this is the day starter you want on the counter at your elbows: a hearty breakfast wrap, filled with eggs, bacon, avocado, cheese, and chili. Perfect food for the perfect life you've chosen—fast and furious and free-spirited, not wrapped tight or buttoned down like the grimly robotic corporate existence you left behind. Or plan to leave behind, someday. That's why so many finance bros from the Exchange come down from their glass towers and cosplay here in biker's leather on weekends. For the burrito!

8 slices thick-cut bacon

2 tablespoons unsalted butter

8 large eggs

Four 10-inch tortillas, warm

1 cup shredded cheddar jack cheese

2 ripe avocados, pitted and diced

1 cup Liberty City MC Chili (page 37), hot

8 tablespoons sour cream

1. Preheat the oven to 425°F. Line a half-sheet pan with aluminum foil, then line up the bacon slices in a single layer, spacing them an inch apart. Bake for 10 minutes, rotate the pan, and bake for 5 to 10 minutes longer, until browned and crisp. Transfer to a paper towel–lined plate and set aside.
2. In a large nonstick skillet, heat the butter over medium-low heat. While the butter melts, in a medium bowl, whisk the eggs until frothy and homogenous. Pour the eggs into the skillet and cook, stirring constantly, until just barely set.
3. Put the tortillas on separate plates. When filling the tortillas, try to keep the ingredients centered. Divide the cheese among the tortillas and top each with the eggs and two slices of bacon. Divide the avocados, chili, and sour cream among the tortillas.
4. To fold and roll the burritos, lift up the left and right sides of them and fold over the filling. While holding the sides down, lift the bottom side of the burrito up and over the filling, then roll the burrito toward the top side, keeping the other sides held down and the filling tightly contained.
5. If desired, heat the burritos, seam-side down, in a clean skillet or griddle over medium-high heat until golden brown and crisp, 3 to 5 minutes. Flip and repeat for the top side of the burrito, then serve hot.

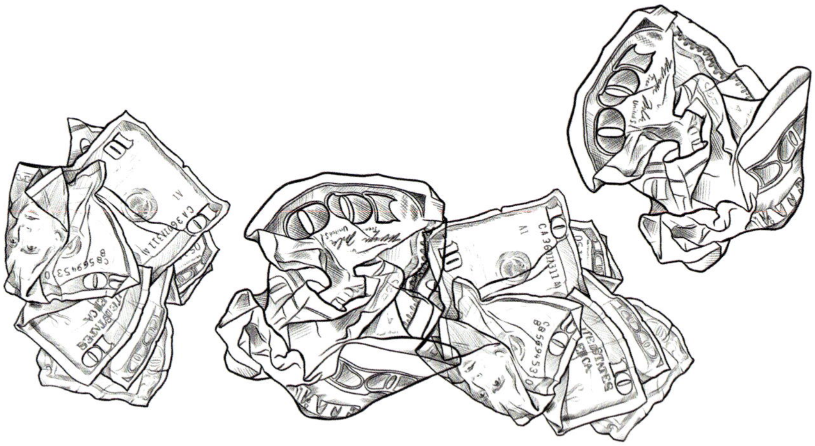

THE LOST & DAMNED BURGER

SERVINGS: 4 | **COOK TIME:** 30 minutes | **DIFFICULTY:** Easy | **DIETARY:** N/A

More than any other single food item, the classic cheeseburger is the one that fuels the American Dream in all its scrabbling, Darwinian, rags-to-riches permutations. Whether you're invested in private equity or a Bohan chop shop—and what's the difference, really?—everybody loves an indulgent burger stacked high with beef, cheese, and all the fixings. That's why the Greasy Chopper thrives. Its Lost & Damned Burger just might be the most quintessentially American food ever devised. Its secrets are in the Damned sauce, the ingenious double-cheese combo, and the innovative smashburger technique. Eat this burger and slay your competitors—metaphorically, of course.

DAMNED SAUCE

¼ cup mayonnaise

¼ cup ketchup

2 tablespoons hot honey

BURGER PATTIES

1½ pounds ground beef

1½ teaspoons kosher salt

1 teaspoon black pepper

1 tablespoon hot sauce

1 teaspoon garlic, minced

1 tablespoon neutral oil

4 slices pepper jack cheese

4 slices smoked cheddar or Gouda

TO ASSEMBLE

4 burger buns or bulkie rolls

4 leaves butter lettuce

4 slices tomato

Pickled jalapeños

1. In a small bowl, stir together the mayonnaise, ketchup, and hot honey. Keep sealed and refrigerated until ready to use.
2. Crumble the ground beef in a large bowl, breaking it up gently with your fingers. Season with the salt, pepper, hot sauce, and garlic. Mix gently until evenly distributed, then divide into eight equal portions. Flatten each portion into a very thin patty.
3. In a large skillet, heat the oil over medium-high heat until shimmering. Add four of the patties, flatten them further with a flat metal spatula, and cook, undisturbed, for 2 to 3 minutes, until well seared. Flip, cook for 1 minute longer, then top with the pepper jack cheese. Transfer the patties to a clean plate, then repeat the process with the remaining patties, topping them with the smoked cheddar.
4. To assemble, divide the buns among four plates. Lay a leaf of lettuce on the bottom of each bun, along with a slice of tomato. Divide the cooked patties among the buns, making sure each burger consists of one patty with pepper jack and one with smoked cheddar. Top with pickled jalapeños and the top half of the bun. Serve with the damned sauce so your guests can use as much or as little as they please.

VICE CITY

Welcome to Vice City, where the 1980s are on a forever loop—vibrant, sun-drenched days cycling into neon nights, over and over into perpetuity. Walking the streets, you feel like an extra in one of those movies with a synth-wave soundtrack by Tangerine Dream. Bold colors, clean lines, big sunglasses, big hair—art deco meets moral ambiguity. And such a melting pot! Ruthless drug lords in pastel suits can openly mingle with corrupt politicians in pastel suits, and . . . vice versa. For many, Vice City is like being in a luminescent coma. There's no waking up. But maybe you don't *want* to wake up.

And then there's the food. Vice City's culinary landscape is as bright as a white sand beach, with eateries that can stand toe-to-toe with any of the great Cuban heavyweights of the era. Look for breezy, laid-back beach fare by day and more upscale cuisine with a cosmopolitan flair by night. In our trio of Vice City restaurants, one features Italian, one Chinese, and one . . . is located on a *yacht*. Yacht dining is the kind of thing Tommy Vercetti would love. It just doesn't get any more Vice City than that, right?

BARZINI'S

With two prime locations—a cozy little spot Downtown, and a more capacious site in the sprawling North Point Mall—Barzini's Ristorante Italiano is as formidable as the illustrious crime family of its namesake. Chandeliers, plush seating, and a sense of casual opulence make this the perfect venue for hosting the hapless targets of your next hostile takeover or gangland assassination. Barzini's entrées are to die for, but the true specials are the world-famous appetizers, sides, and desserts—so here, we present one of each.

CAPRESE DI VICE

SERVINGS: 4 | **COOK TIME:** 10 minutes | **DIFFICULTY:** Easy | **DIETARY:** Vegetarian, Gluten free

The beauty of this dish is its elegant simplicity. There's just no better way to kick off a proxy battle or turf war than with a stunning platter of fresh mozzarella balls (called ciliegine) and vine-ripened cherry tomatoes, drizzled with olive oil and a glaze of balsamic vinegar and then topped with rolled, thinly sliced basil leaves. Served with a splash of Ocean Beach style, it's the kind of starter that can make a common man into a made man.

1 pint cherry tomatoes, halved

8 ounces fresh ciliegine mozzarella, drained and halved

¼ cup basil leaves, rinsed and patted dry with paper towels

1 tablespoon extra virgin olive oil

1 teaspoon balsamic vinegar

1. Put the cherry tomatoes and mozzarella in a medium bowl. Set aside.
2. Stack the basil leaves on top of one another on a cutting board. Roll them up, starting from the long edge, into a tight coil. Slice thinly, crosswise, with a very sharp knife.
3. Drizzle the tomatoes and mozzarella with the olive oil and balsamic vinegar, then toss gently to combine. Top with the basil, toss again to combine, and serve immediately. Caprese salad is best eaten fresh.

PATATE AL ROSMARINO

SERVINGS: 4 to 6 | **COOK TIME:** 1 hour | **DIFFICULTY:** Easy | **DIETARY:** Vegan, Gluten free

Some mob dons make offers you can't refuse. Others—the clever ones—serve up a plate of Barzini's rosemary-infused roasted potatoes, crispy on the outside, soft on the inside, exactly the way you love it. They encourage you to eat, if you know what's good for you. When you finish, you're so grateful that you order a second helping . . . and sign up for the "protection services," no questions asked.

2 pounds fingerling potatoes

3 tablespoons olive oil

1½ teaspoons kosher salt

½ teaspoon black pepper

1 tablespoon finely chopped fresh rosemary leaves

1. Bring a large pot of water to a boil over high heat. Add the potatoes and cook for 15 to 18 minutes, until they are easily pierced by a sharp knife or skewer. Drain and return to the pot, but remove from the heat. Let sit for 5 minutes to allow the potatoes to dry—the residual heat from the pot will help this process.
2. While the potatoes cook, preheat the oven to 450°F and line a half-sheet pan with a sheet of parchment. Once the potatoes are dry, transfer to the sheet pan. Use the bottom of a measuring cup to smash the potatoes down to a thickness of about ½ inch. Don't smash them so they fall apart—you want them to stay intact. Drizzle with the olive oil and season with the salt, pepper, and rosemary.
3. Roast the potatoes for 20 minutes, then flip and roast for 10 to 15 minutes longer, until deep golden brown and crisp at the edges. Serve hot.

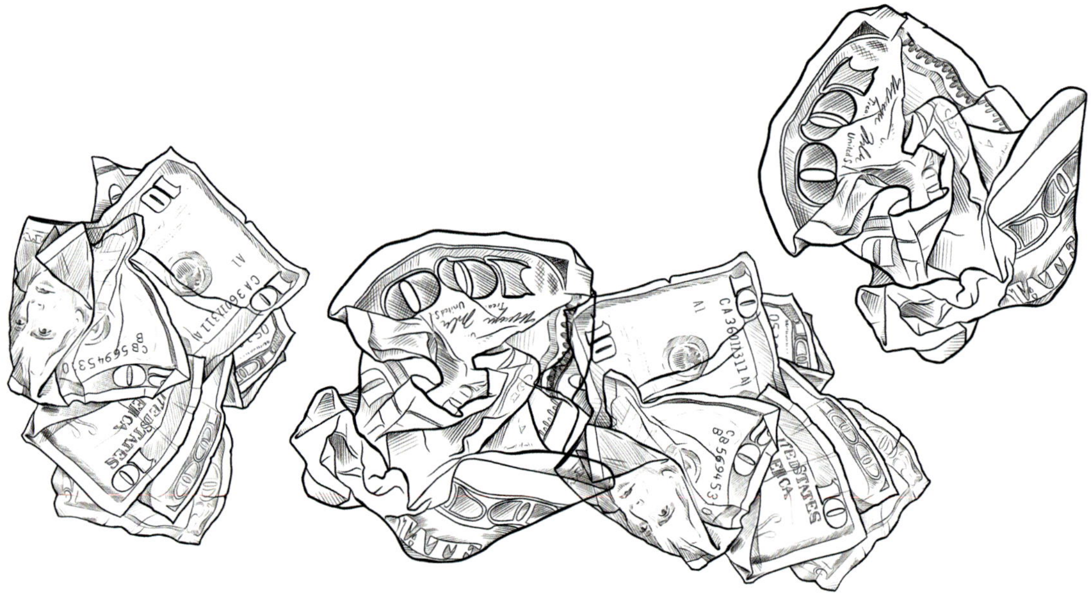

VESUVIUS ALLA BARZINI

SERVINGS: Makes 4 cakes | **COOK TIME:** 15 minutes active, 9 minutes baking | **DIFFICULTY:** Intermediate
DIETARY: Vegetarian

If Mount Vesuvius had tasted like this, the citizens of Pompeii would have welcomed its magma with open arms. This decadent molten lava cake—gooey chocolate erupting with subtle rum and coffee flavorings—put the Barzini clan on the map long before that nasty four-family shootout at the Malibu Club. Note: The dark rum whipped cream is listed as optional, but only if you've completely given up on living the good life.

6 tablespoons unsalted butter, plus more for greasing the ramekins

2 tablespoons cocoa powder

6 ounces dark chocolate, finely chopped

¼ teaspoon kosher salt

¼ teaspoon instant coffee granules

3 large eggs

3 large egg yolks

½ cup dark brown sugar

1 tablespoon dark rum

2 tablespoons all-purpose flour

rum whipped cream (optional)

1 cup whipped cream

1 tablespoon powdered sugar

2 teaspoons dark rum

1. Grease four 6-ounce ramekins with butter, then dust with cocoa powder. Firmly tap out the excess cocoa powder, then set the ramekins on a baking sheet. Preheat the oven to 450°F.
2. Put the chopped chocolate, salt, and coffee granules in a medium heatproof bowl. In a small saucepan, melt 6 tablespoons of butter over medium heat. Cook, swirling occasionally, until the butter solid turns golden brown. Pour the browned butter over the chocolate and set aside to let the chocolate melt.
3. In a separate medium bowl, use a handheld mixer set on medium-high speed to beat together the eggs, yolks, sugar, and rum until thickened and light, 2 to 3 minutes.
4. Stir the chocolate mixture until smooth, then beat in the egg mixture until smooth. Stir in the flour. Divide the batter between the ramekins, then bake for 7 to 9 minutes until just barely set but still slightly jiggly in the center. Let sit for 1 minute before inverting onto separate plates.
5. While the cakes bake, make the whipped cream (if using). In a medium bowl, use a handheld mixer on high speed to beat the heavy cream together with the powdered sugar and rum until soft peaks form, 4 to 6 minutes.
6. Serve the cakes hot with the rum whipped cream or with your favorite ice cream. The cakes go very well with the Cherry Poppers Chocolate Chunk Ice Cream (page 138).

WOK & ROLL

Straight from Hong Kong to the sun-splashed Washington Beach district, this local Chinese food favorite features "seafood, steak, vegetarian, and pasta," as clearly stated on the front window. With its move to America and some clever renaming, Wok & Roll embraced the casual dining atmosphere favored by Vice City denizens. But its dishes are old-school formal in their flavoring and presentation, thanks to the "subtle" influence of the Mountain Master of the Vice City Triads.

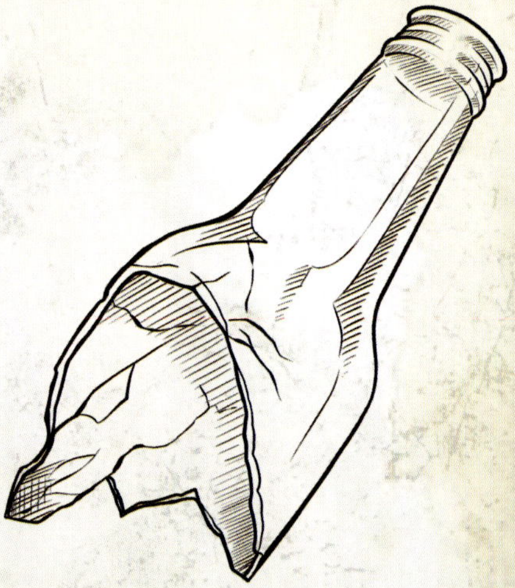

ROCKIN' GENERAL'S CHICKEN

SERVINGS: 4 | **COOK TIME:** 20 minutes marinating, 20 minutes active | **DIFFICULTY:** Intermediate | **DIETARY:** N/A

Some say this dish is named after General Tsung-t'ang, Viceroy of Shaan-gan, a great Chinese statesman and military leader from Hunan Province during the late Qing dynasty. Others say no, it was some other guy. Frankly, this recipe is so good that nobody we know cares. Crispy marinated chicken in a sticky, sweet, and spicy sauce, garnished with crushed peanuts! It most definitely rocks—you feel the General's Fender bass line in the pit of your stomach. Served with a generous side helping of the Rollin' Fried Rice (see the next recipe).

CHICKEN

1 large egg white

2 tablespoons soy sauce

2 tablespoons Shaoxing wine

½ teaspoon baking soda

½ cup cornstarch, divided

1 pound boneless, skinless chicken thighs, cut into 1-inch chunks

1 tablespoon white vinegar

½ cup potato starch

½ teaspoon kosher salt

6 cups peanut oil

SAUCE

¼ cup low-sodium chicken stock

2 tablespoons soy sauce

2 tablespoons Shaoxing wine

2 tablespoons honey

1½ tablespoons white distilled vinegar

1 teaspoon tomato paste

2 teaspoons cornstarch

1 tablespoon water

TO SERVE

Steamed white rice, optional

Rollin' Fried Rice (page 55), optional

CONTINUED ON NEXT PAGE

ROCKIN' GENERAL'S CHICKEN (CONTINUED)

1. Marinate the chicken. In a medium bowl, whisk together the egg white, soy sauce, Shaoxing wine, and baking soda until smooth. Whisk in ¼ cup of cornstarch until smooth, then add the chicken. Toss to coat, stir in the vinegar, and let sit at room temperature for 20 minutes.
2. Meanwhile, in a medium bowl, whisk together the remaining ¼ cup of cornstarch, the potato starch, and kosher salt. Set aside.
3. Prepare the sauce. In a small bowl, combine the chicken stock, soy sauce, Shaoxing wine, honey, vinegar, and tomato paste. Whisk until smooth. In a small bowl, stir together the cornstarch and water, then add this slurry to the chicken stock mixture. Stir to combine and set aside.
4. Drain the excess marinade from the chicken, then transfer the chicken to the bowl with the potato starch mixture from step 2. Toss to coat.
5. Pour the peanut oil into a large wok. Bring to 375°F over medium-high heat. Shake off the excess coating from each piece of chicken and gently lower them into the oil. Cook, gently stirring with a spider strainer or slotted spoon until golden, crisp, and cooked through, 4 to 6 minutes.
6. Transfer the cooked chicken to a paper towel–lined half-sheet pan to drain while you make the sauce.
7. Pour all but 2 tablespoons of the oil from the wok into a heatproof bowl. (You can strain and save the oil to use for another frying project once it cools.)
8. Return the wok to medium-high heat. Add the garlic, ginger, and scallions and cook, stirring constantly, until softened and fragrant, 1 minute. Stir the sauce mixture from step 3, then add it to the wok all at once, along with the dried chiles. Cook, stirring constantly, until the mixture comes to a boil and thickens, 2 to 3 minutes. Stir in the sesame oil, remove from the heat, and add the chicken. Toss to coat and serve immediately with steamed white rice or Rollin' Fried Rice (page 55).

ROLLIN' FRIED RICE

SERVINGS: 4 to 6 | **COOK TIME:** 25 minutes | **DIFFICULTY:** Intermediate | **DIETARY:** Vegetarian

Who doesn't love fried rice packed with veggies, eggs, bean sprouts, and wild mushrooms, all woven together with garlic and spices for a flavor you'll never forget? The correct answer is: nobody. As every Triad chef knows, one secret is to use cold rice, cooked the day before, to avoid the mushiness that is anathema to fried rice lovers. Another tip is to stir-fry your ingredients quickly over medium-high heat. But perhaps the biggest secret is to keep your counterfeit-money-printing plates far away from the wok. It's bad for the rice, and really bad for business.

- 4 tablespoons neutral oil, divided
- 8 ounces wild mushrooms, roughly chopped
- ¼ teaspoon kosher salt
- ¼ teaspoon black pepper
- 4 scallions, thinly sliced
- 2 cloves garlic
- 4 cups cooked long-grain white rice (preferably day-old)
- ½ cup shredded carrots
- ½ cup frozen peas or edamame
- 2 large eggs
- 1 cup bean sprouts
- 3 tablespoons soy sauce
- 2 tablespoons Shaoxing wine

1. In a large wok, heat 2 tablespoons of oil over medium-high heat until shimmering. Add the mushrooms, season with salt and pepper, and cook, stirring occasionally, until browned, 8 to 12 minutes. Transfer to a small bowl and set aside.
2. Add the remaining oil to the wok, along with the scallions and garlic. Cook, stirring constantly, until fragrant, about 1 minute. Add the rice and cook, stirring constantly and breaking up the grains to separate them, then add the carrots and peas. Cook, tossing and stirring constantly, until the rice is warmed through and the carrots and peas are just cooked through, 2 to 4 minutes.
3. Push the rice up the sides of the wok, leaving the bottom clean. Add the eggs to the empty part of the wok and cook, stirring constantly, until they are set. Toss with the rest of the ingredients.
4. Add the bean sprouts and toss to combine. Pour the soy sauce and Shaoxing wine along the walls of the wok. Add the mushrooms. Toss to combine, cooking for 1 minute longer. Serve immediately. Store leftovers in a sealed container in the fridge for up to 5 days.

THE VICE CITY FIRECRACKER

SERVINGS: 1 cocktail | **COOK TIME:** 2 minutes | **DIFFICULTY:** Easy | **DIETARY:** Vegan, Gluten free

People come to Wok & Roll for the food, but they stay for the Firecrackers. This spicy cocktail—made with silver tequila, lime, orange liqueur, and an innovative splash of jalapeño-orange syrup—has just the right amount of kick to match Vice City's late-night ambience. Light the fuse and stand back!

JALAPEÑO-ORANGE SIMPLE SYRUP

1 cup sugar

1 cup water

1 jalapeño, stemmed and coarsely chopped

Zest of 1 orange

COCKTAIL

1 ounce silver tequila

1 ounce lime juice

½ ounce orange liqueur

½ ounce Jalapeño-Orange Syrup

Lime wedge

Jalapeño slice

1. In a small saucepan, combine the sugar, water, jalapeño, and orange zest. Bring to a simmer over medium heat. Remove from the heat, cover, and let steep for 30 minutes. Strain into a heatproof bowl, then cool to room temperature. Transfer to a sealed container and keep chilled for up to 2 weeks.
2. In a cocktail shaker filled with ice, add the tequila, lime juice, orange liqueur, and syrup. Shake for 30 seconds, then strain into a margarita glass filled with ice. Garnish with a lime wedge and jalapeño slice and serve immediately.

BENNY'S RESTAURANT

Welcome aboard the boat where every meal is a happy voyage! This high-end dining establishment is tucked in a truly unique location—the top two decks of a luxurious superyacht, moored on the Little Havana shoreline just off Bayshore Avenue. For years, Benny's has been the place where Vice City's power elite feed on steak, seafood, and one another's hearts. Who owns this yacht? Nobody knows. And, apparently, nobody wants to know. (It's possibly the kind of knowledge that can kill you.) Come to think of it, nobody knows who Benny is, either. But it's Benny's Restaurant, and it's as fine a venue as you'll ever patronize in south Leonida.

OCEAN BEACH SURF & TURF

SERVINGS: 2 | **COOK TIME:** 1 hour | **DIFFICULTY:** Easy | **DIETARY:** Gluten free

Let's start with the menu's superstar entrée, shall we? The Ocean Beach Surf & Turf is a power move on a plate, the city's favorite enabler of rapacious schemes. A perfectly grilled 10-ounce steak is shrewdly paired with blackened, spice-rubbed jumbo shrimp, all drizzled with a smoky rum glaze that truly sweetens the deal. This meal is so potently delicious, it's been known to defenestrate lesser men.

TURF

Two 10-ounce boneless ribeye or NY strip steaks

2 teaspoons neutral oil

1½ teaspoons kosher salt

1 teaspoon black pepper

SURF

½ teaspoon kosher salt

1 teaspoon smoked paprika

½ teaspoon dried thyme

½ teaspoon dried oregano

¼ teaspoon garlic powder

¼ teaspoon black pepper

Pinch cayenne (or more, if you like some heat)

8 ounces peeled jumbo shrimp

2 tablespoons olive oil

RUM SAUCE

2 tablespoons olive oil

2 cloves garlic, minced

1 small shallot, minced

½ cup dark rum

1 teaspoon fresh thyme leaves (or ½ teaspoon dried)

1 tablespoon red wine vinegar

2 tablespoons unsalted butter, cubed

1. Prepare the steaks for the grill. Pat the steaks dry with a paper towel, then brush all over with a thin layer of the oil. Season both steaks with salt and pepper, then set aside on a plate to come to room temperature for 20 minutes or so.
2. Prepare the rub for the shrimp. In a small bowl, whisk together the salt, paprika, thyme, oregano, garlic powder, black pepper, and cayenne until well combined. Pat dry the shrimp with paper towels and toss with the spice rub until well coated. Keep in the fridge until ready to cook.
3. Meanwhile, prepare your grill or broiler. **If using a charcoal grill:** Fill a chimney starter with charcoal, then pack the bottom with newspaper or crumpled brown paper bags. Light the starter and wait for the coals to light all the way through. The coals are ready to use once they are glowing and coated in ash. While the coals light, brush a thin layer of neutral oil on the grill grate (or spray with cooking spray meant for use with a grill). Dump the coals in an even layer on the bottom of your grill. Place the grill grate over the coals, cover the grill, and allow to preheat for about 5 minutes. **If using a gas grill:** Oil the grates, light the burners on high, and allow the grill to preheat for about 5 minutes. **If using a broiler:** Place an oven rack directly under the broiler.
4. **If using a grill:** Place the steaks over the hottest part of the grill and cook for 3 to 4 minutes, until well seared with grill marks and light char. Flip and cook for 2 to 3 minutes longer. Transfer to a cutting board, lightly tent with foil, and let rest in a warm place for 10 to 15 minutes. **If using a broiler:** Place the steaks on an oven-safe wire cooling rack set in a half-sheet pan (or a broiling pan if you have one). Place the pan in the oven so the steaks are directly under the flame and cook for 3 to 4 minutes until well seared. Flip and cook for 2 to 3 minutes longer. Transfer to a cutting board, lightly tent with foil, and let rest for 10 to 15 minutes.

CONTINUED ON NEXT PAGE

OCEAN BEACH SURF & TURF (CONTINUED)

5. While the steaks rest, cook the shrimp. In a large stainless-steel skillet, heat 2 tablespoons of olive oil over medium-high heat until shimmering. Add the shrimp in a single layer and let cook, undisturbed, until well seared, 2 to 3 minutes. Flip and cook for 2 to 3 minutes longer, until opaque all the way through. Transfer to a heatproof bowl and keep in a warm place.
6. Wipe out the pan with a paper towel, pour 2 tablespoons of olive oil into the pan, and place back over medium-high heat. Add the garlic and shallots and cook, stirring constantly, until softened and fragrant, 1 to 2 minutes.
7. This next part can be tricky and slightly dangerous. If you're comfortable with flambéing, add the rum and tilt the pan toward the flames to ignite the rum. Let the flames die down naturally and let the rum boil down until it's reduced by about half, 2 to 3 minutes. Stir in the fresh thyme, vinegar, and butter, then cook, stirring constantly, until a glossy, emulsified sauce forms, about 1 minute. If you're NOT comfortable with flambéing, remove the pan from the heat once the garlic and shallots are soft and fragrant. Carefully pour in the rum, then return the pan to a medium flame. Bring the mixture to a simmer and let simmer until reduced by half—it will take a bit longer with the lower flame. Once the rum is reduced by half, add the thyme, vinegar, and butter and stir until a glossy, emulsified sauce forms.
8. Divide the steaks and shrimp between two plates, drizzle with the rum sauce, and serve immediately.

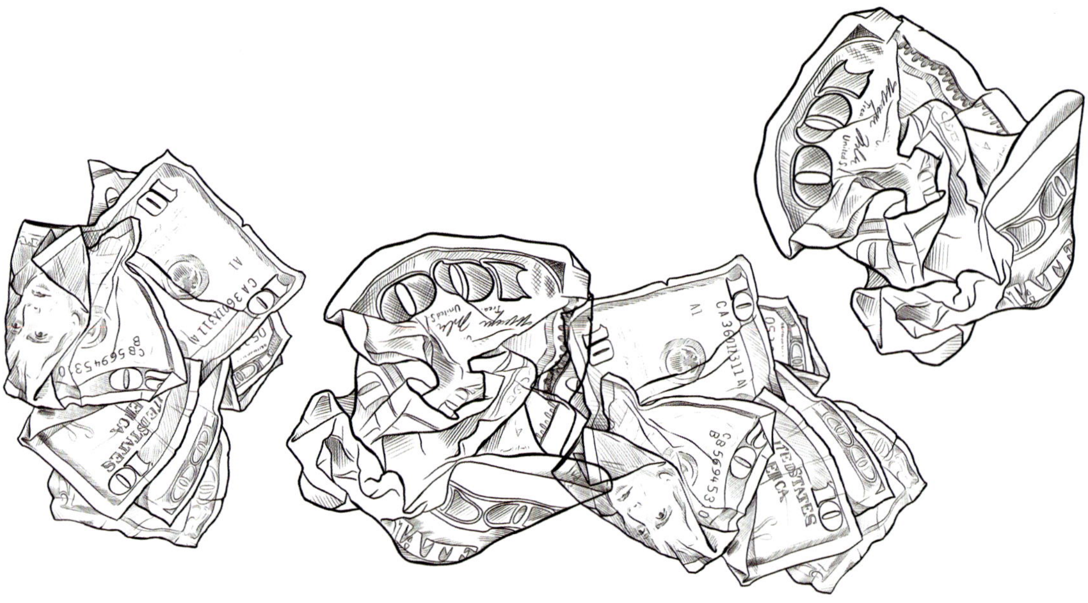

THE CAPTAIN'S KEY LIME PIE

SERVINGS: 8 to 10 | **COOK TIME:** 20 minutes active, 6 hours 50 minutes cooling and chilling
DIFFICULTY: Easy | **DIETARY:** Vegetarian

If you're going to dine aboard a superyacht, you must have the captain's pie. But not just any pie. This is the great state of Leonida, where "pie" is short for "key lime pie," the iconic confection invented in the Gator Keys somewhere south-ish of Vice City. Swamp folk call it the devil's dessert. Of course, everything seems demonic in a swamp—because, you know, it's a swamp—but these people have a point. At Benny's, the key lime pie is so ridiculously good, it just has to be evil.

CRUST

1¼ cups graham cracker crumbs

¼ cup finely shredded toasted coconut

¼ teaspoon kosher salt

2 tablespoons granulated sugar

6 tablespoons unsalted butter, melted and cooled

FILLING

One 14-ounce can sweetened, condensed milk

4 large egg yolks

½ cup key lime juice (fresh or bottled)

1 teaspoon finely grated key lime zest (or regular lime zest if using bottled juice)

1 teaspoon vanilla extract

COCONUT WHIPPED CREAM

1½ cups heavy cream

3 tablespoons powdered sugar

1 teaspoon vanilla extract

½ teaspoon coconut extract

½ teaspoon lime zest

1. Preheat the oven to 375°F. Put the graham cracker crumbs, coconut, salt, and sugar in the bowl of a food processor. Pulse to combine and further break down the coconut, 2 to 3 minutes, then tip the contents of the food processor into a medium bowl. Stir in the melted butter until thoroughly mixed.
2. Press the crust mixture into the bottom and up the sides of a 9-inch pie plate (don't use a deep-dish pie plate for this—if that's all you have, you can also use a 9-inch springform pan and just press the crust mixture up the sides of the pan to a height of about 1 inch). Press firmly to compress the piecrust. Chill for at least 20 minutes.
3. Bake the piecrust for about 10 minutes, until just a few shades darker all over and golden brown at the edges. Set aside to cool as you prepare the filling. Reduce the oven temperature to 325°F.
4. In a medium bowl, whisk together the sweetened, condensed milk, egg yolks, key lime juice, zest, and vanilla until smooth and creamy, about 2 minutes. Pour into the crust and bake for 12 to 15 minutes, until just the very center of the filling jiggles when gently shaken. Let cool at room temperature for 30 minutes, then cover and chill for at least 6 hours.
5. When ready to serve, make the coconut whipped cream. In a large bowl with an electric handheld mixer on medium-high speed, beat the heavy cream, powdered sugar, vanilla, and coconut extract until stiff peaks form. Dollop all over the top of the pie and smooth into an even layer. Scatter lime zest over the top of the whipped cream, slice, and serve. Keep leftover pie covered and chilled for up to 3 days.

THE PINK FLAMINGO COCKTAIL

SERVINGS: 2 | **COOK TIME:** 3 minutes | **DIFFICULTY:** Easy | **DIETARY:** Vegan, Gluten free

Behold this mischievous two-rum concoction, as easy to mix as it is frivolous and fun to drink. Simply blend your two rums (white and coconut) with frozen strawberries, lime, and coconut cream, then garnish exuberantly with a pink flamingo straw. (*Exuberance* is really the key here.) But be sure to sip your cocktail very, very slowly . . . because every tiny moment of pleasure must be savored while you remain unmurdered in Vice City.

2 cups frozen strawberries

1 cup coconut milk

2 ounces coconut rum

2 ounces white rum

1 ounce lime juice

1 ounce cream of coconut

Pink flamingo straws

1. In the bowl of a blender, combine the strawberries, coconut milk, coconut run, white rum, lime juice, and cream of coconut. Blend on low, gradually increasing the speed to high, blending for a total of about 2 minutes, until smooth.
2. Pour into two glasses and serve with pink flamingo straws.

LOS SANTOS

The rest of the world often equates Los Santos with Vinewood and Rockford Hills, as if the film industry was the only thing going on in the City of the Saints. But L.S. is a sprawling basin metropolis of many districts, filled with millions of people in diverse cultures and industries. Sure, they make movies here. It's a celebrity-based civilization with 75 miles of beachfront coastline. Money grows on trees; so does overnight fame. But let's not forget the city's truly impressive array of organized criminal activities, including some of the world's most notoriously big street gangs—e.g., The Families and the Ballas down in the South Los Santos projects. This sun-bleached conurbation is a mecca for drug trafficking, extortion, robbery, back-alley "transactions," and other fun, lucrative business.

For our purposes, it's important to point out that Greater Los Santos also boasts one of the most dynamic food scenes anywhere—a true melting pot of cuisines flavored by the city's rich history of immigration waves. From fine dining to health-conscious "clean eating" (local and sustainable!) to playful fusion cuisines (sushi burritos, anyone?) to its vibrant street food culture, Los Santos is a hotbed for culinary experimentation. Sitting on the coast, the city is also a seafood superstar. Let's check out a few of our favorite dishes, shall we?

LA SPADA

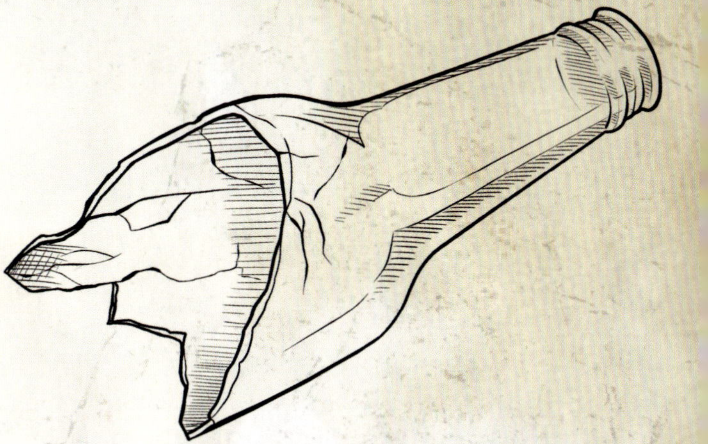

Billing itself as an Italian Style Seafood Restaurant, La Spada can be found near the intersection of Aguja and Goma Streets in the La Puerta district of Los Santos, a proud blue-collar community with strong roots in the fishing, longshoring, and industrial cement industries. This restaurant features vibrant recipes infused with the essence of Italian coastal cuisine. As its name suggests, La Spada's signature specialty is swordfish. It's also famous for its killer shrimp. And its killers. The local Armenian mob loves to celebrate its "victories" here.

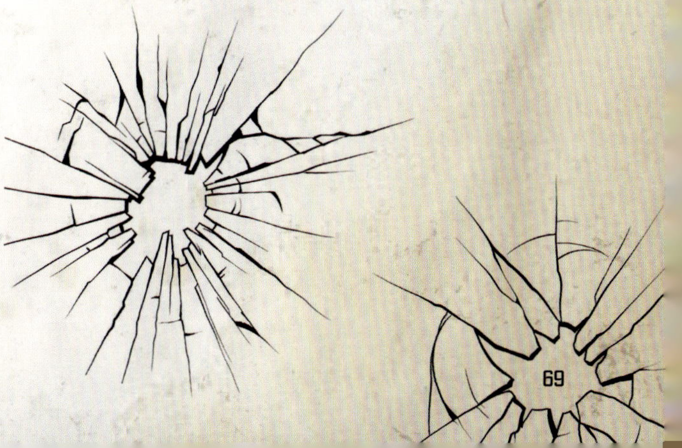

COZZE ALLA MARINARA

SERVINGS: 4 | **COOK TIME:** 25 minutes | **DIFFICULTY:** Easy | **DIETARY:** Gluten free

Popular not only in Italy but across Northern Europe too, this briny delicacy can serve as a great starter or a side dish. Cozze, of course, is Italian for "mussels," and the recipe's roots trace back centuries to the seafaring traditions of Italian fishermen and sailors. These shellfish must be very fresh—alive, in fact!—and well-scrubbed. The fun part is tearing off their "beards," the tough, silky bundle of filaments called the byssus that each mussel secretes from its shell. (Mussels use these to attach to solid surfaces underwater.) Once the mussels are cooked, be sure to serve the cooking sauce too, which is perfect for dipping with crusty bread.

2 pounds mussels, shells scrubbed, rinsed, and beards removed

2 tablespoons olive oil

2 small shallots, thinly sliced

4 cloves garlic, thinly sliced

1 large sprig thyme

½ cup vermouth

½ cup Italian white wine, such as pinot grigio or trebbiano

2 tablespoons cold unsalted butter, cubed

TO SERVE

Warm, crusty Italian bread

1. Check the mussels to make sure they're all alive. Any mussels that are either cracked or do not close when tapped should be discarded. Set aside in a bowl.
2. In a large pot, heat the oil over medium heat, then add the shallots and garlic. Cook, stirring constantly, until softened and fragrant, 2 to 5 minutes. If you find the garlic or shallots are browning, reduce the heat.
3. Add the thyme, vermouth, and wine. Increase the heat to high and bring to a boil. Cook, stirring occasionally, until the liquid is reduced by about half. Add the mussels and cover the pot. Open after 1 minute, stir and toss the mussels, cover, and repeat until the mussels have all opened up. This should only take 3 to 5 minutes, total. If, after 5 minutes, there are any mussels that haven't opened up, discard them.
4. Transfer the mussels to a serving bowl using a slotted spoon or wire spider strainer. Return the pot to the heat and stir the butter into the cooking liquid, stirring constantly to emulsify the sauce. Once the butter has melted and the sauce is shiny, homogeneous, and slightly thickened, pour all over the mussels. Serve immediately with crusty bread.

RISOTTO CON L'ARAGOSTA

SERVINGS: 4 to 6 | **COOK TIME:** 30 minutes | **DIFFICULTY:** Intermediate | **DIETARY:** Gluten free

You probably know that risotto is a creamy Italian rice dish typically made with short-grain rice like (in this case) Carnaroli, slow cooked in an exquisitely flavored stock. But we're extremely happy to report that L'aragosta is Italian for "lobster," which should make everyone you feed very happy too—yes, this creamy, comforting dish is made with fresh lobster meat. This is easily one of La Spada's most popular entrées, and the recipe is less tricky than it might appear at first glance. Indeed, it's the kind of recipe taught in the finest culinary schools as a sneaky way to boost confidence (and enrollment).

1 pound steamed lobster meat

6 to 8 cups seafood or lobster stock

2 tablespoons olive oil

4 tablespoons unsalted butter

1 small leek, finely chopped (white and light green parts only)

2 cups carnaroli rice*

¼ cup brandy

¾ cup freshly grated Parmesan

*Note: If you can't find carnaroli rice, arborio rice will work well!

1. Pick through the lobster meat and reserve the best-looking four to six claws (use as many as you need for the people you're serving). Chop the remaining lobster meat.
2. Pour the stock into a medium pot and place over medium-low heat to keep hot.
3. In a large sauté pan with high walls, heat the oil and butter over medium-high heat until foaming. Add the leek and cook, stirring constantly, until softened, 2 to 4 minutes. Add the rice and cook, stirring constantly, until the grains just start to become opaque, 2 to 4 minutes.
4. Stir in the brandy and 1 cup of the stock. Cook, stirring gently and constantly, until the liquid has been totally absorbed. Continue this process, adding a cup of stock at a time and stirring until it is totally absorbed, until the rice is tender, 20 to 25 minutes longer. Note that you may not use all of the stock before the rice is ready to eat.
5. Stir in ½ cup of Parmesan cheese and all the lobster meat except for the reserved claws. Remove from the heat and let sit just long enough for the lobster meat to warm through, 1 to 2 minutes.
6. Divide the risotto between shallow bowls, topping each portion with a good pinch of the remaining Parmesan and a reserved lobster claw.

BRANZINO AL FORNO

SERVINGS: 4 | **COOK TIME:** 30 minutes | **DIFFICULTY:** Intermediate | **DIETARY:** Gluten free

This amazing oven-baked European sea bass is a Mediterranean classic—a tender, flaky whitefish that pairs perfectly with simple, fresh ingredients. Very popular in Italian cuisine as a main course, branzino can be served as a whole-fish presentation to showcase its cultural roots and impress your local neighborhood don. (It might even earn you a bit of extra protection.) La Spada's Chef Lorenzo shared this advice for your fish-market trip: "Fresh branzino should have a nice sheen and clear eyes." So, there you have it.

4 branzino, gutted, scaled, dorsal fins removed

2 tablespoons olive oil

2 teaspoons kosher salt

1 teaspoon black pepper

1 lemon, halved and thinly sliced

8 sprigs fresh oregano

8 sprigs fresh dill, plus 1 tablespoon finely chopped dill

6 tablespoons salted butter

1. Preheat the oven to 425°F. Line a half-sheet pan with parchment paper. Pat dry the fish with paper towels, then rub all over with the olive oil. Season inside and out with the salt and pepper.
2. Place the fish on the prepared sheet pan. Make three angle slits on both sides of each fish—cut through the skin and into the flesh, but be careful not to cut all the way through the flesh. Pack each fish with three or four slices of lemon and two sprigs each of the oregano and dill.
3. Roast the fish for 10 minutes, then very carefully flip with a thin fish spatula and roast for 10 to 15 minutes longer, until the flesh is very easily pierced with a small knife. Serve immediately.

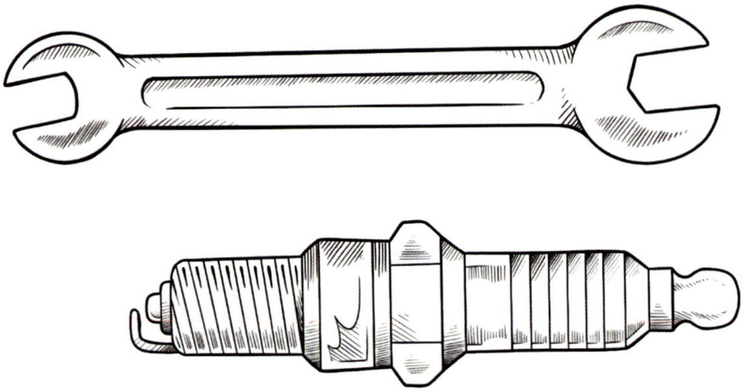

NUTSAKI

This upscale Japanese restaurant is a hotspot off San Andreas Avenue near the Prosperity Street Promenade in the trendy beachfront community of Del Perro—a place where beach bums live better than most Americans. Nutsaki features a stylish mix of traditional and modern Japanese dishes with the occasionally quirky twist. Not quite as quirky as the restaurant logo, however, which pays artistic homage to sand-level views at certain secluded beaches below the Palomino Highlands.

LYCHEE SAKETINI

SERVINGS: 1 | **COOK TIME:** 5 minutes | **DIFFICULTY:** Easy | **DIETARY:** Vegan, Gluten free

This elegant Japanese variation on the martini takes less than five minutes to make, but its salubrious effects may just last a lifetime. Two parts nigori sake, one part gin, plus your lychee flavors and a bit of elbow grease for the shaking. Nutsaki's head bartender, Akira, shared his famous technique with us: After you fill the shaker with ice and ingredients, secure its lid with both hands then shake horizontally over your shoulder. Do so with a fluid, rhythmic, slightly twisting motion while counting slowly to ten until the shaker frosts up. Pour in a chilled glass, drink, and contemplate everything profoundly.

1. In a cocktail shaker filled with ice, add the sake, gin, lychee juice, and lychee syrup. Shake vigorously until the outside of the shaker becomes frosty.
2. Strain into a cocktail glass. Thread the lychee fruit onto a metal cocktail spear and set over the rim of the glass so the lychee hovers over the cocktail.

2 ounces nigori sake

1 ounce gin

1 ounce lychee juice

Splash lychee syrup

1 lychee fruit, canned

TERIYAKI CHICKEN

SERVINGS: 4 | **COOK TIME:** 30 minute marinating, 20 minutes active | **DIFFICULTY:** Easy | **DIETARY:** N/A

Some might see this tried-and-true dish as a venerable but slightly boring staple of international versions of Japanese dining. While true at many places, not so at Nutsaki. The restaurant's remarkable rendition of this grilled chicken specialty is glazed with a sweet and savory teriyaki sauce—a sauce so good and yet so easy to make, you'll think that ancient Shinto spirits cast their yōkai magic on your simple ingredients. When served with steamed rice and broccoli, this dish tastes exactly like a perfect sunset on the Seto Inland Sea.

1½ tablespoons dark brown sugar

2 teaspoons cornstarch

¼ cup soy sauce

2 tablespoons mirin

2 tablespoons pineapple juice

1 tablespoon grated ginger

1½ pounds skinless, boneless chicken thighs, cut to 1-inch chunks

2 tablespoons neutral oil

2 teaspoons toasted sesame oil

TO SERVE

Steamed white rice

Steamed broccoli

1. In a small bowl, whisk together the brown sugar and cornstarch until combined. Add half the soy sauce and whisk until smooth. Whisk in the remaining soy sauce, along with the mirin, pineapple juice, and ginger. Chill in the fridge for 30 minutes.
2. Drain the marinade from the chicken, being sure to reserve all of the marinade. In a large wok, heat the neutral and sesame oils over medium-high heat until shimmering. Add the chicken all at once, spreading it into a single layer. Let cook, undisturbed, until well seared, 3 to 5 minutes.
3. Continue cooking the chicken, stirring constantly, until cooked through, 2 to 4 minutes longer. Add the reserved marinade to the wok and continue stirring until the sauce comes to a boil and thickens, coating the chicken, 2 to 3 minutes longer.
4. Serve the chicken over steamed white rice with steamed broccoli.

MATCHA CHEESECAKE

SERVINGS: 8 to 12 | **COOK TIME:** 30 minutes active, 4 hours chilling | **DIFFICULTY:** Easy | **DIETARY:** Vegetarian

Matcha, as you may know, is a powdered form of green tea featured in many Japanese tea ceremonies. It's known to be an antioxidant powerhouse, legendary for the health benefits it bestows. But it also adds a wonderfully zesty burst to all kinds of dessert recipes—in particular, it pairs perfectly with the creamy sweetness of a cheesecake. Nutsaki's version uses a ceremonial grade matcha powder for its filling—make sure you do the same, as it adds a more robust flavor. Don't skip past the strawberry whipped cream for the topping. The sheer majesty of this cream cheese–matcha-strawberry flavor blend rivals that of even Mount Fuji.

CRUST

1½ cups graham cracker crumbs

4 tablespoons unsalted butter, melted

FILLING

2 tablespoons ceremonial grade matcha powder, sifted

3 tablespoons hot water

One 8-ounce package cream cheese, softened

¾ cup powdered sugar

2 teaspoons vanilla extract

1 cup heavy cream

STRAWBERRY WHIPPED CREAM

½ cup freeze-dried strawberries

3 tablespoons powdered sugar

2 cups heavy cream

1. In a small bowl, stir together the graham cracker crumbs and butter until fully moistened. Pack this mixture into the bottom of an 8-inch springform cake pan, compressing as best you can with your fingers, then pressing well with the flat bottom of a drinking glass or measuring cup. Chill while you prepare the filling.
2. In a small bowl, stir together the sifted matcha powder and hot water until a completely smooth paste forms. Make sure there are no clumps of matcha left—if needed, add up to one more tablespoon of hot water to thin the mixture out. Set aside.
3. In a medium bowl with an electric handheld mixer, beat the cream cheese until smooth and creamy, 3 to 5 minutes. Beat in the matcha paste, powdered sugar, and vanilla until smooth, 4 to 6 minutes longer.
4. In a separate bowl with an electric mixer (you can use a stand mixer for this if you have one), whip the heavy cream to stiff peaks. Fold the heavy cream into the cream cheese mixture until fully incorporated. Pour over the crust, smoothing it out to an even layer. Cover the pan and chill while you make the whipped cream.
5. Put the freeze-dried strawberries and powdered sugar in the bowl of a food processor. Process until finely powdered, then, with the processor running, stream in the heavy cream. Process for 1 minute, scrape the sides down, then process for 30 to 60 seconds longer until smooth and thick. Pour the whipped cream over the matcha cheesecake. Cover and chill for at least 4 hours. Keep leftovers covered and chilled for up to 5 days.

LETTUCE BE

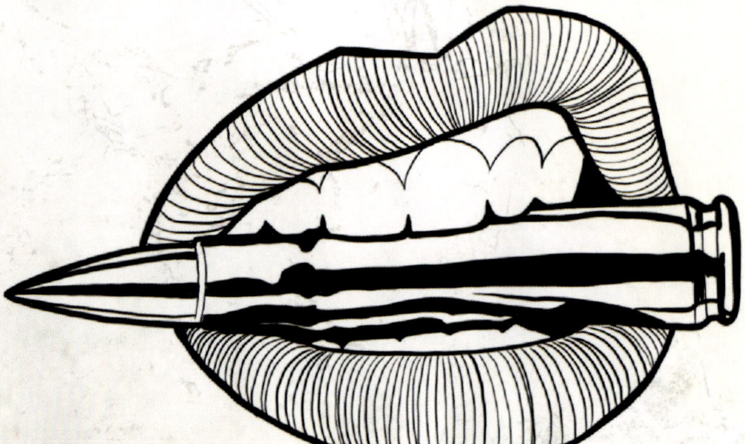

Really, what could rep the trendy, health-conscious Los Santos lifestyle better than a vegetarian restaurant chain? If you crave "eco-friendly décor and a non-toxic ambiance," you can find Lettuce Be franchises in the Hawick, Del Perro, and Vespucci Canals districts. Each features exactly the kind of organic, farm-to-table cuisine you'd expect from an eatery so devoted to the West Coast vibe. But if you can stomach green walls adorned with neo-hippie slogans, you'll find the food quite amazing. Or skip all the virtue-signaling and just whip these up in your own kitchen. Check out the lip-smacking recipes that follow.

OH KALE YEAH! BOWL

SERVINGS: 4 | **COOK TIME:** 45 minutes | **DIFFICULTY:** Easy | **DIETARY:** Vegan, Gluten free

This delicious, kale-packed bowl of superfood is designed to fuel a busy morning of yoga, meditation, and hustling the awards circuit for your studio. The recipe is fun and easy to make. After you roast and season your chickpeas, just assemble the kale, quinoa, diced avocado, and salted pepitas in a bowl. Add the chickpeas and top with a smooth, tasty tahini dressing, freshly made and lightly sweetened with agave or maple. You'll find the subtle blend of flavors almost as tasty as the fortune you made betting on the ponderous sci-fi space opera that all the smart people said was doomed to fail.

ROASTED CHICKPEAS

1 can chickpeas, drained and rinsed

2 tablespoons olive oil

½ teaspoon kosher salt

½ teaspoon smoked paprika

½ teaspoon lemon zest

¼ teaspoon black pepper

¼ teaspoon garlic powder

¼ teaspoon onion powder

TAHINI DRESSING

½ cup tahini

2 tablespoons lemon juice

2 tablespoons white wine vinegar (or apple cider vinegar)

¼ cup water

1 tablespoon agave syrup or maple syrup

½ teaspoon kosher salt

¼ teaspoon black pepper

TO ASSEMBLE

4 cups kale, chopped, tough stems removed

1 tablespoon olive oil

4 cups cooked quinoa

2 avocados, diced

1 cup roasted, salted pepitas

1. Preheat the oven to 425°F. Gently rub the chickpeas with a clean kitchen towel or paper towels to dry them and remove their skins, then discard the skins. In a medium bowl, toss the chickpeas with olive oil to coat, then season with the salt, paprika, lemon zest, pepper, garlic powder, and onion powder. Roast for 20 to 30 minutes, until crisp. Let cool and keep stored in a sealed container at room temperature for up to 3 days.
2. In a medium bowl, mix together the tahini, lemon juice, and vinegar until smooth. The tahini will seize up at first, but just keep mixing—it will eventually relax and blend easily with the other liquids. Add the water, agave, salt, and pepper, and keep mixing until smooth. The dressing can be made ahead and will keep in the fridge for up to 1 week.
3. Put the kale in a large bowl along with the olive oil. Massage vigorously with your hands until it feels noticeably tender. Divide among four large salad bowls.
4. Add the quinoa to the bowls, then top with the diced avocado, roasted chickpeas, and salted pepitas. Serve with the tahini dressing.

DIRTY GREEN SMOOTHIE

SERVINGS: Two 16-ounce smoothies | **COOK TIME:** 4 minutes | **DIFFICULTY:** Easy | **DIETARY:** Vegan, Gluten free

In Los Santos, it seems like everybody's "detoxing" yet nobody's happy about it. Wouldn't it be great to find a detox smoothie recipe that not only packs a health punch, but tastes great? If that seems like a foodist oxymoron, well, Lettuce Be has just the thing for you. The restaurant's signature Dirty Green Smoothie cleanses, energizes, kickstarts your immune system, supports organ function, blah blah blah, all that nonsense—and yet it tastes suspiciously indulgent. An ingenious blend of ingredients creates the perfect combination of clean and "dirty" (as in, damn, that's tasty). Soon you can't live without it. Because nothing's more addictive than being both smug and healthy.

1 cup ice

1 cup almond milk (or other nut- or plant-based milk)

1-inch piece ginger, peeled

1 small avocado, pitted and diced

1 cup packed baby spinach

1 large banana, peeled and roughly chopped

1 cup chopped pineapple

4-inch piece of seedless cucumber, roughly chopped

1. In the bowl of a blender, combine the ice, almond milk, ginger, avocado, spinach, banana, pineapple, and cucumber.
2. Blend on low, gradually increasing the speed to high, blending for a total of 1 to 2 minutes, until smooth and creamy.
3. Divide between two glasses and serve immediately.

VEGAN LAVENDER LEMONADE

SERVINGS: 1½ quarts | **COOK TIME:** 20 minutes, 30 minutes cooling | **DIFFICULTY:** Easy | **DIETARY:** Vegan, Gluten free

People go to great lengths to achieve peak health in Los Santos. An important but often underrated enabler of that state is the art of finding simple joy. This refreshing, lightly sweet drink, made with a brilliant blend of lavender-agave syrup and fresh lemon juice, is one of those things that inspires people to sit contentedly in the very place they inhabit at that very moment and think: I like it here, right now. Please leave me alone.

1 cup sugar

1 cup water

1 tablespoon dried lavender buds

¼ cup agave syrup

1 cup lemon juice

4 cups water

1. In a small saucepan, combine the sugar, water, and lavender buds. Bring to a boil over high heat, then cover and remove from the heat. Let steep for 15 minutes, then strain into a heatproof bowl.
2. Whisk in the agave syrup and let cool at room temperature for 30 minutes.
3. In a large pitcher, stir together the lavender syrup, lemon juice, and water. Serve over ice. Keep lemonade chilled for up to 1 week.

LAST TRAIN IN LOS SANTOS DINER

Gleaming red on Eclipse Boulevard in West Vinewood, this wonderful little diner is comprised of two old-school passenger rail carriages. Last Train is a hipster favorite, but don't let that drive you away—the locals and diner staff may be desperate to claw their way into the entertainment industry, but the food they serve is truly outstanding! And with plenty of parking out back, Last Train knows exactly how to cater to its clientele, the most car-dependent culture on the planet. (Just be sure to tip the valet . . . or you may run afoul of his red glow stick.)

VINEWOOD GLAM OMELETTE

SERVINGS: 2 | **COOK TIME:** 15 minutes | **DIFFICULTY:** Easy | **DIETARY:** Gluten free

Some say this dish was Bogart's favorite after a long day on the set. Others insist it was his favorite before a long day on the set. The pointless debate rages in the film industry to this very day. Whatever the case, this astounding omelette is as glam as Vinewood itself. Healthy yet indulgent, with bold flavors and a cinematic flair—eggs, red onion, red pepper, diced ham, fresh chopped baby spinach, and a quarter-cup kick of feta cheese. Mix extra-virgin olive oil with a touch of butter for decadent richness in your skillet. And that's a wrap, folks!

4 large eggs

½ teaspoon kosher salt, divided

2 tablespoons unsalted butter, divided

1 tablespoon olive oil

½ cup diced ham

¼ cup diced red bell pepper

2 tablespoons diced red onion

¼ teaspoon black pepper

1 cup finely chopped baby spinach

2 ounces feta, crumbled

1. In a small bowl, whisk the eggs and ¼ teaspoon of kosher salt until frothy and homogenous. Set aside.
2. In a large, nonstick skillet, heat 1 tablespoon of butter and the olive oil over medium-high heat until melted and foaming. Add the ham, bell pepper, and onion and cook, stirring occasionally, until the bell pepper and onion are softened, 5 to 7 minutes. Reduce the heat to medium-low. Add the spinach, season with the remaining ¼ teaspoon of salt and the pepper, and cook, stirring occasionally, until wilted and bright green, 2 to 3 minutes.
3. Add the remaining 1 tablespoon of butter, whisk the eggs for 30 seconds, and add them to the skillet. Cook, stirring vigorously, until the eggs just barely start to set. Spread the eggs into an even layer and cover. Cook for 2 to 4 minutes, until the eggs are just about totally set. Crumble the feta over the omelette, remove the pan from the heat, and cover. Let sit for 1 minute, until the cheese is warmed and the eggs are completely set. Use a thin spatula to fold the omelette in half, then carefully slide onto a large plate. Serve immediately.

LOS SANTOS MILKSHAKE AND HAPPY DUST DONUTS

SERVINGS: 2 | **COOK TIME:** 5 minutes | **DIFFICULTY:** Easy | **DIETARY:** Vegetarian, Gluten free

This quaint railcar diner may be the "last train in Los Santos," but it will always be the first destination for the notorious dessert junkies in West Vinewood's movie industry. This famous milkshake is timeless, like Ingrid Bergman's ethereal glow in *Casablanca* and the iconic Wilhelm screams heard across the sets at Richards Majestic Productions. These addicts have a keen nose for the finest white powder this side of the Bolivian jungle. Coated generously on golden-brown donuts fresh from the oven, Los Santos Diner's happy dust has always been the perfect pick-me-up after a long hard day of clapping the slate on the studio lot. (We're talking about sugar here, people. What's wrong with you?)

CINNAMON WHIPPED CREAM

½ cup heavy cream

1 tablespoon powdered sugar

¼ teaspoon cinnamon

MEXICAN HOT CHOCOLATE MILKSHAKE

1 pint vanilla ice cream

½ cup milk

¼ cup chocolate syrup

½ teaspoon cinnamon

1 pinch chili powder

2 maraschino cherries

DONUTS

4 tablespoons unsalted butter, softened

¼ cup neutral oil

½ cup light brown sugar

¼ cup granulated sugar

2 large eggs, room temperature

1½ teaspoons baking powder

½ teaspoon baking soda

1 teaspoon kosher salt

1 teaspoon ground cinnamon

¼ teaspoon ground nutmeg

2 teaspoons vanilla extract

2½ cups all-purpose flour

1 cup whole milk, room temp

1 cup powdered sugar

TO MAKE THE MILKSHAKE

1. In a medium bowl with an electric handheld mixer, beat together the heavy cream, powdered sugar, and cinnamon until stiff peaks form. Keep chilled until ready to use.
2. Put the vanilla ice cream, milk, chocolate syrup, cinnamon, and chili powder in the bowl of blender. Cover and blend on low, gradually increasing the speed to high, blending for a total of 1 to 2 minutes, until smooth.
3. Divide the milkshakes between two chilled tall glasses. Top each with a big dollop of whipped cream and a cherry.

TO MAKE THE DONUTS

1. Heat the oven to 375°F. Lightly grease two donut pans.
2. Beat together the butter, oil, brown sugar, and sugar in a large bowl until lightened in color and smooth. Beat in the eggs until thick and creamy, 2 to 4 minutes. Beat in the baking powder, baking soda, salt, cinnamon, nutmeg, and vanilla extract.
3. Gently mix in about half the flour, followed by all of the milk, stirring just until combined, then stir in the remaining flour until no dry streaks of flour remain. Transfer the donut batter to a large piping bag, then snip the tip to make a roughly 1-inch hole.
4. Pipe the batter into the donut pan, filling each mold about ¾ full. There should be roughly ¼ inch of space left at the tops of each mold. Give the pans a quick tap or two on the counter to knock out any excess air.
5. Bake the donuts for 11 to 13 minutes, until golden brown and the tops spring back when you gently press them.
6. Let the donuts cool in the pan for about 5 minutes before turning out onto a wire rack to cool.
7. Add the powdered sugar to a zip-top plastic bag. While the donuts are still just warm, but not hot, add them one at a time and shake to coat with the powdered sugar. Serve warm. These donuts are best eaten on the day they're made, but can be stored at room temperature in a sealed container for up to 2 days. Note that the powdered sugar will melt into the donuts after a few hours.

LAS VENTURAS

Built on the shifting desert sands of human frailty, Las Venturas is where the American Dream morphs into a mutant parody of itself—a neon-lit facade erected on a dark web of ruination. Folks don't pull up their bootstraps here; they throw dice, trying to get rich quick. As the famous gonzo journalist once put it, "Venturas is what it is—a place where excess and depravity come together and get celebrated." It's a city where the lines between reality and illusion blur.

And hey, it's also a great family vacation spot! The mob spent billions to clean up the streets, making everything bright and shiny—a place Mom can hit the spa, Dad the casino, Uncle Ted the brothels, and the kids run like packs of coyotes through the amusement parks. Plus, you can eat quite well here. Food is tasty and plentiful and remarkably inexpensive, often financed by the house take in the casinos. Check out our recipe offerings from the three first-rate eateries.

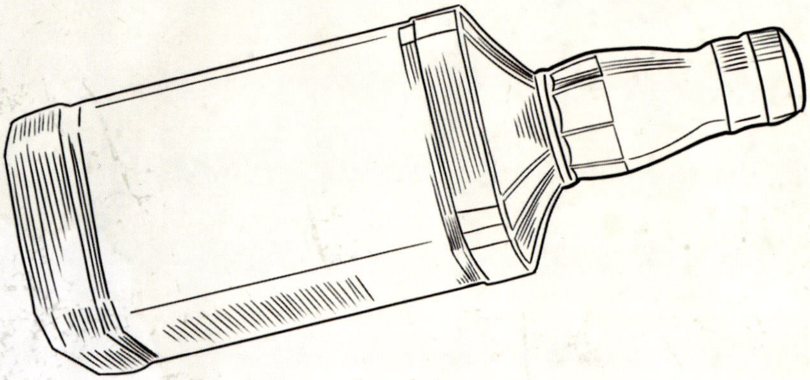

WORLD OF COQ

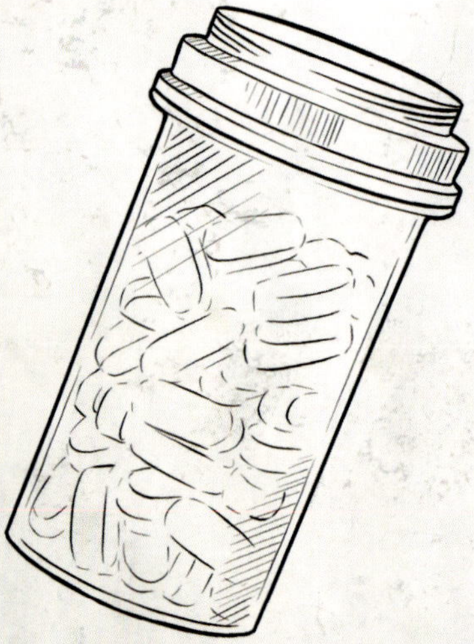

This upscale, fine-dining experience is part of a three-venue chain founded by French chef Richard "Dick" Goblin, the legendary restauranteur and onetime host of the popular (and remarkably grisly) Coq O Vin cooking show on Liberty City Free Radio. Goblin's Las Venturas venue is in the Old Venturas Strip district. (The other two Coq venues are in the cities of San Fierro and Los Santos.) With some of the finest French cuisine this side of Lyon, World of Coq is the perfect place to wine and dine your date after hitting 22 straight up at roulette. C'est délicieux!

GOUGÈRES

SERVINGS: 6 to 8 | **COOK TIME:** 45 minutes | **DIFFICULTY:** Intermediate | **DIETARY:** Vegetarian

Here's a classic French appetizer. If you're not familiar with the term, a gougère is a savory French pastry made of choux (a delicate dough) mixed with cheese and then baked to golden brown. The dough prep takes some work, but it's fun to display your Coq technique as you wield the saucier and wooden spoon. Don't be put off by the dough's webby, gluey consistency in the mixing bowl—the steam released in the oven will transform it into a remarkably delicate, puffy pastry.

1. In a medium saucepan or saucier, combine the milk, butter, sugar, salt, and nutmeg. Bring to a boil over high heat. Remove from the heat and vigorously stir in the flour with a wooden spoon until smooth.
2. Return the saucepan to high heat and continue stirring vigorously until the mixture reaches an internal temperature of 170°F.
3. Dump the mixture into the bowl of a stand mixer fitted with a paddle attachment. Beat on medium heat until the temperature drops to 145°F or lower. Start taking the temperature after about 3 minutes, then continue beating for 1 minute at a time until the correct temperature is reached.
4. Add the eggs one at a time, beating at medium speed until fully incorporated before adding the next egg. Once all the eggs are in, stop the mixer, scrape down the sides, add the shredded Gouda and half the Parmesan, and beat on medium speed for another 5 to 10 seconds until fully mixed.
5. Preheat the oven to 400°F and line a half-sheet pan with parchment.
6. Transfer the gougères batter to a large piping bag fitted with a large star tip. To keep the parchment from moving as you work, pipe a small blob of gougères batter under all four corners of the parchment.
7. Pipe four rows of five gougères each onto the prepared parchment paper. Sprinkle with the remaining Parmesan, then bake for 20 minutes, until golden brown. Turn off the oven and prop it open with a serving spoon or spatula. Let cool for another 20 minutes, then serve the gougères warm or at room temperature. Store leftover gougères in a sealed container in the fridge for up to 5 days. Reheat on a parchment-lined pan at 350F° for 5 to 10 minutes, or until crisp.

1 cup whole milk

6 tablespoons unsalted butter, cubed

1 teaspoon kosher salt

Pinch nutmeg

1 cup all-purpose flour

4 large eggs

4 ounces shredded Gouda

2 ounces freshly grated Parmesan, divided

CHICKEN PROVENÇAL

SERVINGS: 6 to 8 | **COOK TIME:** 20 minutes active, 40 minutes roasting | **DIFFICULTY:** Easy | **DIETARY:** Gluten free

World of Coq shares its namesake's fascination with the tender thighs of a hen. This French delicacy is a fancy, flavorful dish featuring browned, bone-in chicken thighs braised with tomatoes, olives, shallots, garlic cloves, lemon, white wine, and herbes de Provence. Pay attention to our recipe's last sentence—mopping up the braise with a warm baguette is one of those surprising little dining moments so flavorsome you'll never forget it.

6 to 8 skin-on, bone-in chicken thighs

1 tablespoon kosher salt

2 teaspoons black pepper

2 tablespoons olive oil

1 cup grape tomatoes

½ cup pitted green olives (such as castelvetrano)

1 large lemon, cut into eighths

2 medium shallots, peeled and quartered

8 cloves garlic, peeled

1 cup dry white wine

2 teaspoons herbes de Provence

TO SERVE

Warm baguette

Cooked rice

Mashed potatoes

1. Preheat the oven to 400°F. Pat dry the chicken thighs with paper towels, then season all over with salt and pepper.
2. Pour the oil into a large cast-iron or stainless-steel skillet or braising pan (12 inches is ideal, and you must use something oven-safe for this). Heat over medium-high heat until shimmering. Place the chicken thighs in the pan skin-side down and cook, undisturbed, for 2 minutes, then reduce the heat to medium and cook for 5 to 7 minutes longer, until the skin is crisp and golden brown.
3. Flip the thighs over and allow them to cook while you arrange the remaining ingredients in the pan. Tuck the grape tomatoes, olive, lemon, shallots, and garlic in between the chicken thighs, distributing these ingredients evenly throughout the pan. Pour in the white wine, then season the entire contents of the pan, thighs and all, with the herbes de Provence.
4. Place the pan in the oven, uncovered, and roast until the thighs are cooked through and register 165°F when an instant-read thermometer is inserted into the thickest part of the thighs. Serve in the pan alongside the starch of your choice. The braising liquid is especially delicious when mopped up with a piece of warm, crusty baguette, but white rice or mashed potatoes are also great accompaniments.

CRÈME BRÛLÉE AU COQ

SERVINGS: 4 | **COOK TIME:** 30 minutes active, 40 minutes baking, 6 hours 20 minutes cooling and chilling
DIFFICULTY: Intermediate | **DIETARY:** Vegetarian, Gluten free

Nothing is more wonderfully self-indulgent than this soft custard dessert with the crackly crust of caramelized sugar. Crème brûlée defines an entire era of French hegemony in haute cuisine. The base recipe and its name—French for "burned cream"—first appeared in a Parisian cookbook back in 1691. But it wasn't until the 1980s that crème brûlée became the darling of every upscale eatery, thanks to its popularity at the world-famous Le Cirque restaurant (with its tagline: "Where art, fashion and food converge"). As you might expect, World of Coq has its own Las Venturas–style take on the classic.

3 cups heavy cream

1 vanilla bean

8 egg yolks

¼ teaspoon kosher salt

½ cup granulated sugar, plus 4 teaspoons

½ teaspoon vanilla extract

1. Pour the heavy cream into a medium saucepan. Split the vanilla bean in half lengthwise, scrape out the seeds, and add the seeds and pod to the heavy cream. Place over medium heat and bring to a bare simmer, then remove from the heat, cover, and let steep for at least 20 minutes. (You can also steep overnight in the fridge for a deeper vanilla flavor—just heat back up over medium heat until it just starts to steam before proceeding.)
2. Preheat the oven to 325°F. Remove the vanilla bean pod from the heavy cream. In a small bowl, gently whisk together the egg yolks, ½ cup of sugar, and the salt. Add a splash, about a couple of tablespoons, of the cream to the egg mixture and whisk. Whisk gently and constantly, while adding the cream a splash at a time, until you've added about half the cream, then add the remaining cream in a slow, steady stream until it's been completely incorporated.
3. Place a fine-mesh strainer over a large, spouted measuring cup or mixing bowl. Strain the custard from step 2 into the measuring cup and discard any solids.
4. Place a paper towel at the bottom of a 9-by-13-inch cake pan, then line up four 8-ounce ramekins in a 2-by-2 pattern on top of the paper towel (the paper towel will help keep the ramekins from sliding around). Divide the custard among the ramekins. Fill the cake pan with boiling water so it reaches about halfway up the sides of the ramekins. Use a kitchen torch or stick lighter to very gently heat the tops of the crème brûlées to burst any tiny bubbles leftover from whisking.
5. Loosely cover the cake pan with foil and bake for 35 to 40 minutes, until just the very centers of the crème brûlées jiggle slightly when you gently shake the pan. (Be especially gentle so you don't accidentally splash water into the crème brûlées!)
6. Remove the crème brûlées from the water and let cool on the countertop or a wire cooling rack for about 20 minutes before covering them individually with foil or plastic wrap and chilling for at least 6 hours or up to 3 days.
7. When ready to serve, add about 1 teaspoon of sugar to the tops of each custard, then carefully heat with a kitchen torch until the sugar melts and caramelizes. Wait about 1 minute for the sugar to harden before serving immediately. (If you intend to have leftovers, don't do this step until you're ready to serve; otherwise, the sugar will take on moisture and lose its signature crackly crunch.)

STAUB
STAUB
STAUB

CALIGULA'S CASINO BUFFET

Gambling on stuff is fun, but when you're hungry, you want a sure bet. At Caligula's Palace Hotel & Casino, the all-you-can-eat buffet offers a mix of dishes that you can always count on. A Las Venturas mainstay for more than three decades, Caligula's houses the largest hotel in the world and is possibly the mobbiest casino as well—some say three different East Coast crime families "co-own" the place, whatever that means. The casino buffet features a cornucopia of delights . . . although the ridiculously low prices don't even come close to offsetting your gambling losses.

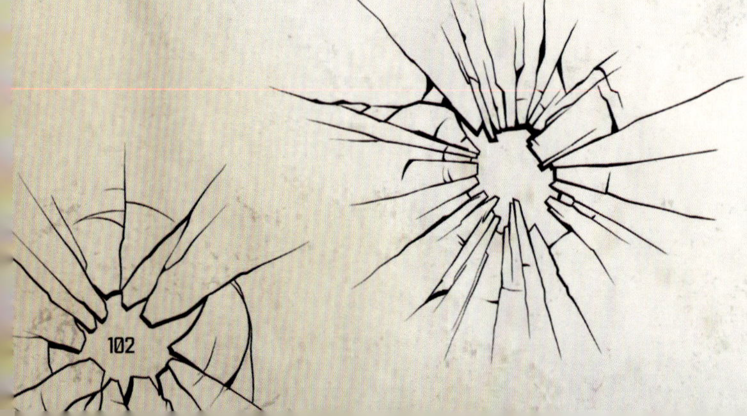

GLADIATOR'S GOLD SHRIMP COCKTAIL

SERVINGS: 4 to 6 | **COOK TIME:** 15 minutes, plus cooling time | **DIFFICULTY:** Intermediate | **DIETARY:** Gluten free

The great Spartacus once led a bloody revolt at the gladiator school in Capua because of subpar chow, or so the rumor goes. In the Caligula's Casino kitchen, strict gladiator rules apply—only the very best recipes survive to be served. Here's one of the buffet's biggest winners: jumbo shrimp, succulent, served in Caligula's signature cocktail sauce made of citrus-infused golden grape tomatoes. Any Roman emperor, no matter how capricious, would give it the immediate thumbs-up.

GOLDEN COCKTAIL SAUCE

1 pint golden grape tomatoes, roughly chopped

1 tablespoon prepared horseradish

1 teaspoon kosher salt

½ teaspoon black pepper

¼ teaspoon garlic powder

¼ teaspoon onion powder

1 teaspoon honey

Juice of 1 lemon

SHRIMP

2 pounds jumbo shrimp, peeled and deveined

½ teaspoon baking soda

1 tablespoon seafood seasoning

2 tablespoons kosher salt

1. In a small saucepan, cook the tomatoes and water over medium heat, stirring occasionally, until the tomatoes break down and release their juices. Continue cooking, stirring frequently, until the tomatoes reduce to a thickened sauce, 10 to 15 minutes total. Remove from the heat and let cool for 10 minutes.
2. Transfer the tomato sauce to a food processor, along with the horseradish, salt, pepper, garlic powder, onion powder, honey, and lemon juice. Pulse to combine into a thick sauce. Taste and adjust the seasoning as desired. Transfer to a small bowl, cover, and chill for at least 3 hours.
3. Put the shrimp in a small bowl and toss with the baking soda and seafood seasoning. Chill in the fridge for 20 minutes.
4. Transfer the shrimp to a medium pot, along with 2 quarts of cold water and the kosher salt. Place over medium-high heat and cook, stirring occasionally, until the water comes to just the barest of simmers and the shrimp are cooked through. The shrimp may become cooked through before the water simmers—if that happens, go ahead and strain the shrimp through a colander (the shrimp will be done cooking once they are completely opaque all the way through). Run cold water over the shrimp until they're cool to the touch, then drain them completely. Serve with the golden cocktail sauce.

THE HIGH ROLLER SOUFFLÉ

SERVINGS: 4 to 6 | **COOK TIME:** 15 minutes active, 35 minutes baking | **DIFFICULTY:** Hard | **DIETARY:** Vegetarian, Gluten free

Nothing says Roman decadence quite like a dark chocolate soufflé. This opulent confection usually "rises" to the occasion . . . but to be honest, it sometimes falls flat too. Just remember that a collapsed soufflé still tastes great; it just doesn't look as cool. Whether your soufflé ends up fluffy or deflated, it's still an emperor's feast. And yes, chef: Whatever happens, don't be deflated yourself. The High Roller Soufflé is one of the trickiest recipes in this cookbook.

8 ounces dark chocolate, coarsely chopped (70% cacao or higher)

8 tablespoons unsalted butter, plus 1 tablespoon for soufflé dish

½ teaspoon instant coffee granules

2 teaspoons vanilla extract

6 large eggs, separated

½ teaspoon kosher salt

¼ teaspoon cream of tartar

½ cup granulated sugar, plus 2 tablespoons for soufflé dish

TO SERVE

Vanilla ice cream (optional)

Whipped cream (optional)

Cherry Poppers Chocolate Chunk Ice Cream (pg 138) (optional)

1. Place an oven rack in the lowest position, then preheat the oven to 400°F.
2. Put the dark chocolate and butter in the bowl of a double boiler (or a heat-proof mixing bowl set over a small saucepan of simmering water, making sure the bottom of the bowl isn't touching the water). Melt the chocolate and butter together, stirring constantly, until smooth.
3. Stir in the coffee granules and vanilla and cool for 2 to 5 minutes until the mixture is warm but not hot. Beat the egg yolks into the chocolate mixture until smooth. Set aside.
4. In the bowl of a stand mixer fitted with the whisk attachment, beat together the eggs, salt, and cream of tartar on low until foamy, then increase to medium speed and beat to soft peaks. With the mixer still running, add the sugar a little bit at a time and continue beating until the mixture is glossy with stiff peaks.
5. Scoop about one-quarter of the egg whites into the chocolate mixture and stir it in to loosen it up. Fold in half of the remaining egg whites until no streaks remain, then fold in the remaining egg whites.
6. Coat the bottom and inner sides of a 1½-quart soufflé dish with 1 tablespoon of softened butter, then sprinkle in 2 tablespoons of granulated sugar. Tilt and spin the dish to coat the entire inside with the sugar, then tap out the excess sugar.
7. Carefully pour the soufflé batter into the soufflé dish. Run your finger or an offset spatula between the rim of the dish and the batter to create a small gap, then place the soufflé in the oven. Lower the temperature of the oven to 375°F and bake for 30 to 35 minutes, until the top of the soufflé looks dry and the very center jiggles slightly when you gently shake the dish. Serve immediately with vanilla ice cream, whipped cream, or Cherry Poppers Chocolate Chunk Ice Cream.

TOCINO DE CIELO

SERVINGS: 8 to 12 | **COOK TIME:** 30 minutes active, 80 minutes baking, 6 hours chilling
DIFFICULTY: Hard | **DIETARY:** Vegetarian, Gluten free

This is technically a Spanish dessert. But in Emperor Caligula's time, Hispania—the Roman name for the Iberian Peninsula—was one of many provinces in the firm grip of Roman rule. Thus, it still fits into the casino's theme of imperial decadence . . . lavish, indulgent, sinful. Similar to flan but made without milk, tocino de cielo arises from the simplest of ingredients: egg yolks, sugar, and water. However, as with the previous soufflé recipe, a patient approach is required. Note: It may seem odd that tocino de cielo translates to "bacon from heaven" even though no bacon is involved. But history suggests the name traces to the pudding's resemblance to pork fatback.

2 cups granulated sugar, divided

½ cup water plus 2 tablespoons, divided

3 cinnamon sticks

2-inch piece lemon peel

4-inch piece orange peel

10 large egg yolks

1. In a small stainless-steel saucepan, combine ½ cup of sugar and 2 tablespoons of water over medium-high heat. Cook, gently swirling the pan occasionally, until the sugar caramelizes and turns a dark amber color. Immediately remove from the heat and pour into the bottom of an 8-by-4-inch bread pan. Tilt the pan so that the caramel completely coats the bottom. You'll need to work quickly, as the caramel will start to harden. Set aside (and don't be alarmed if the caramel starts cracking).
2. In a medium saucepan, combine the remaining 1¾ cups of sugar, ½ cup of water, the cinnamon sticks, lemon rind, and orange rind. Place over medium-high heat and cook, swirling the pan occasionally, until the mixture bubbles and turns sticky and syrupy, reaching a temperature between 225°F and 230°F. Remove from the heat and let cool to at least 145°F.
3. In a medium bowl, whisk the egg yolks until smooth. Remove the cinnamon sticks and lemon and orange rinds from the sugar mixture. While whisking gently and constantly, slowly add the syrup a little bit at a time until it's fully incorporated. Whisk until smooth, then strain the mixture through a fine-mesh strainer, discarding any solids.
4. Pour the egg mixture into the bread pan and cover tightly with foil. Place in a 9-by-13-inch cake pan or large roasting pan. Fill the baking dish with boiling water until it rises to about the halfway point on the bread pan. Bake for 70 to 80 minutes, until the tocino de cielo just slightly jiggles when shaken gently.
5. Remove the bread pan from the water bath and let cool at room temperature for 30 minutes before transferring to the fridge to chill for at least 6 hours.
6. Run a thin knife around the edge of the tocino de cielo to loosen it from the edges of the pan. Dip the bottom of the pan into a larger pan or bowl of hot water, holding the pan down in the water (but not submerging it completely—just enough to match the level of the tocino de cielo) for about 15 seconds.
7. Dry the bottom of the pan, place a long, rectangular plate over the top of the bread pan, then invert the pan. The tocino de cielo should fall on its own after a few seconds. Just let it sit for a few minutes and gravity should do the work for you. If not, hold the pan and plate together with your hands and give it a sharp, downward shake to help loosen it from the pan. It should slip out with a satisfying plop.
8. Cut the tocino de cielo into ¾- to 1-inch slices and serve. Leftovers should be covered tightly and kept chilled for up to 3 days.

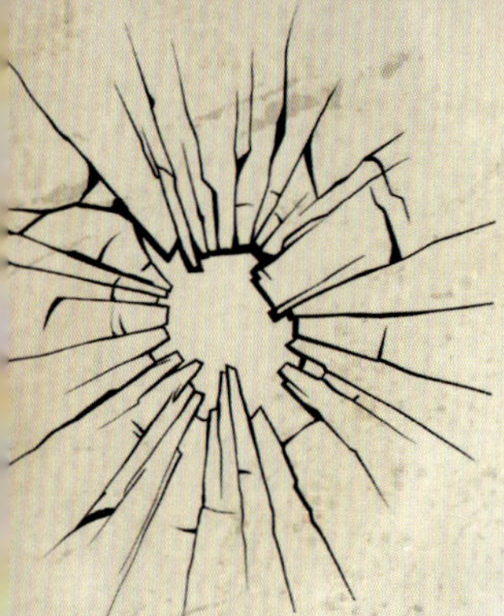

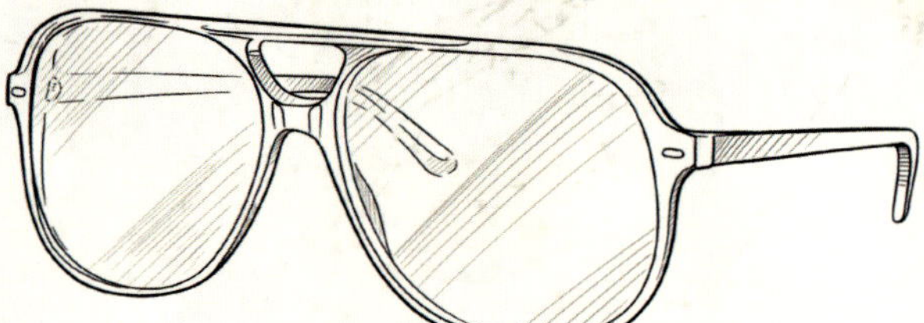

LA LOBA ROJA

Once saddled with the truly pedestrian name of the Mexican Restaurant, this newly christened and exquisitely themed restaurant can be found in the Redsands East district, just across the diagonal from Las Venturas Fire Station No. 3 above the Harry Gold Parkway. La Loba Roja—which translates to "the red wolf," a cool name if ever there was one—serves up a modern twist on classic Mexican dishes. This place is perfect for risk-taking adventurers (a nice euphemism for "inveterate gamblers") who want to enjoy bold flavors under the neon glow of Las Venturas, where hope and tequila both flow like the desert winds.

CHILES RELLENOS DE TRUFFLE

SERVINGS: 4 | **COOK TIME:** 1 hour active, 20 minutes baking | **DIFFICULTY:** Intermediate | **DIETARY:** Vegetarian, Gluten free

Roasted poblano peppers are one of nature's greatest gifts to mankind: El gran regalo de la naturaleza. Think of them as perfect edible vessels to fill with stuffings (called rellenos) made of stunning food combos. At La Loba Roja, Chef Miguel chars these mild chile peppers and stuffs them with onion, beans, and a creamy truffle-infused goat cheese. Then he serves it on a bed of freshly made charred corn salsa. We've seen patrons literally weep with gratitude. You may too.

8 poblano peppers

2 tablespoons olive oil

1 small yellow onion, minced

2 cloves garlic, minced

½ teaspoon kosher salt

½ teaspoon black pepper

½ teaspoon ground cumin

½ teaspoon ground coriander

¼ teaspoon dried Mexican oregano (or dried marjoram)

1 cup canned black beans, drained and well-rinsed

8 ounces truffle goat cheese, room temperature

4 ounces Oaxaca cheese, shredded

CORN SALSA

2 tablespoons olive oil

1 red bell pepper, diced

1 small yellow onion, finely chopped

¾ teaspoon kosher salt

½ teaspoon black pepper

2 cups frozen fire-roasted corn

1 pint grape tomatoes, diced

1 serrano pepper, seeded and minced

½ bunch cilantro, finely chopped

Juice of 1 lime

1. Place an oven rack directly under the broiler, then turn on the broiler. Put the poblano peppers on a half-sheet pan, then broil directly under the flame for 10 to 15 minutes, turning often, until the peppers are well charred all over. The timing will depend on the strength of your broiler, so keep checking on the peppers as you work.
2. Remove the peppers from the oven and transfer them to a heatproof bowl. Cover the bowl and let them steam and cool for 15 minutes.
3. While the peppers steam, prepare the filling. In a large skillet, heat the oil over medium-high heat until shimmering. Add the onion and cook, stirring occasionally, until softened and beginning to turn brown around the edges, 6 to 9 minutes. Add the garlic, salt, black pepper, cumin, coriander, and Mexican oregano and cook, stirring constantly, until fragrant, about 1 minute.
4. Add the beans and cook, stirring and tossing occasionally, until warmed through, 2 to 4 minutes. Remove from the heat and transfer to a bowl to cool.
5. Place an oven rack in the center position and preheat the oven to 425°F. Uncover the poblano peppers and, working with one at a time, run them under cold water and carefully peel off the charred skin. Make a slit along the length of each pepper and remove the seeds and membranes. Pat dry with paper towels and line them up in a lightly oiled large casserole dish or an 9-by-13-inch baking dish.

CONTINUED ON NEXT PAGE

CHILES RELLENOS DE TRUFFLE (CONTINUED)

6. Crumble the goat cheese over the bean mixture, then add the Oaxaca cheese. Toss to combine, then taste the filling—adjust the seasoning with more salt and black pepper if needed.
7. Pack each pepper with as much of the filling as will fit (3 to 4 tablespoons or so, depending on the size of the peppers)—you may end up with left-over filling. Return the peppers, filling-side up, to the baking dish and cover with foil. Add ¼ cup of water to the bottom of the pan, just enough to barely cover the bottom of the dish with a thin layer of water. Bake for 15 to 20 minutes, until the cheese is melted and the filling is warm. Then uncover the baking dish and bake for 5 minutes longer.
8. While the peppers bake, prepare the roasted corn salsa. In a large skillet, heat the oil over medium-high heat until shimmering. Add the bell pepper and onion and cook, stirring occasionally, until softened and the onions begin to turn brown at the edges, 7 to 10 minutes. Season with salt and black pepper, then add the corn.
9. Continue cooking, stirring and tossing occasionally, until the corn is warmed through and tender, 4 to 6 minutes. Add the tomatoes and serrano pepper and cook, stirring and tossing occasionally, until warmed through, 2 to 3 minutes. Remove from the heat, then stir in all but a good pinch of the cilantro and all of the lime juice. Season to taste with additional salt and black pepper if needed.
10. Divide the corn salsa among four shallow bowls, top with two of the cooked peppers, and garnish with a sprinkle of chopped cilantro. Serve hot.

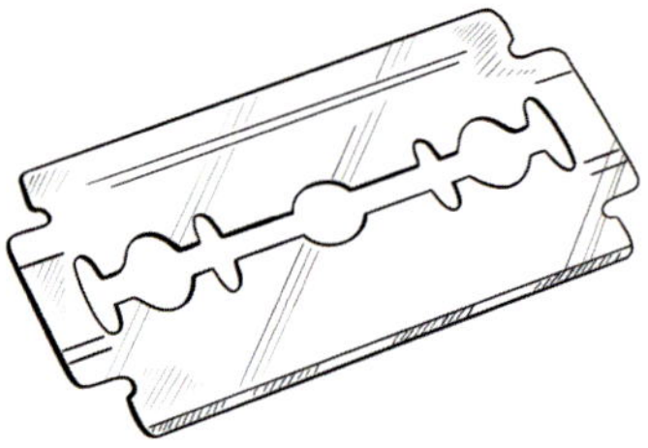

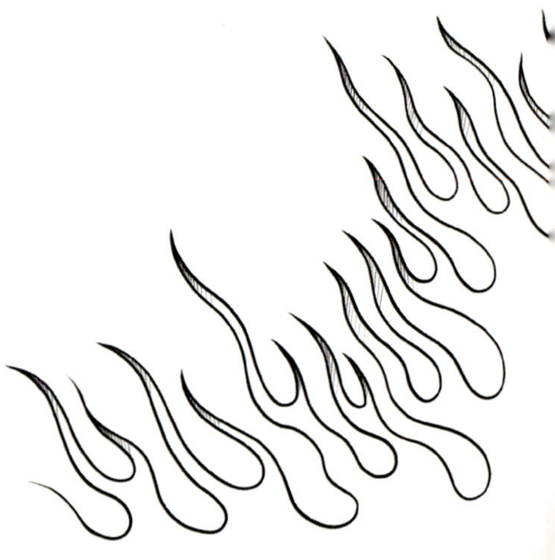

TACOS DE COCHINITA PIBIL

SERVINGS: 6 to 8 | **COOK TIME:** 20 minutes active, 4 hours marinating, 4 hours cooking
DIFFICULTY: Easy | **DIETARY:** Gluten free

Yes, gambling can be an addiction. But in Las Venturas, it's entirely possible to responsibly divert some of that compulsion into the addictive Mexican dishes available at La Loba Roja. For example: These tacos are stuffed with a traditional Yucatec Mayan barbecued pork called *cochinita pibil*, marinated in achiote then slow-roasted. (The name translates as "piglet cooked underground" because the Mayans did their roasting in pits.) The tacos are served with pickled red onions, avocado salsa verde, and a drizzle of Mexican crema. This is substantial food, amigos. And you're here for the high stakes, not the small bites, right?

COCHINITA PIBIL

1 large grapefruit

1 large orange

3 limes

6 cloves garlic, peeled

¼ cup achiote paste

4 teaspoons kosher salt

1 tablespoon ground cumin

2 teaspoons black pepper

2 teaspoons ground coriander

1 teaspoon cinnamon

½ teaspoon ground allspice

½ teaspoon ground clove

4 pounds boneless pork shoulder, cut to 3-inch chunks

1 medium yellow onion, thinly sliced

2 large banana leaves, optional

AVOCADO SALSA

6 large avocados, pitted and diced

1 cup jarred salsa verde

½ teaspoon kosher salt

Juice of 2 limes

TO SERVE

Warm corn tortillas

Pickled red onions

Shredded Oaxaca cheese

Mexican crema

1. Using a juicer, juice the grapefruit, orange, and limes into a small bowl. Put the juice in the bowl of a blender, along with the garlic, achiote paste, salt, cumin, pepper, coriander, cinnamon, allspice, and clove. Blend until smooth.
2. Put the pork in a large bowl. Cover with the marinade, tossing to coat. Seal the bowl and refrigerate for 4 to 8 hours. When ready to cook, preheat the oven to 300°F.
3. If using banana leaves: Lay the banana leaves in a cross shape. Mount the pork up in the center of the banana leaves, then wrap the banana leaves around the pork to form a tight packet. Use butcher twine to secure the banana leaves. Place the packet in a large Dutch oven, plus 1 cup of water. Cover and roast for 3 to 4 hours, until the pork is tender. If not using the banana leaves: Place the pork into a large casserole and cover tightly with tin foil. Roast for 3 to 4 hours, until the pork is tender. Remove the pork from the cooking liquid and transfer to a bowl. Shred the pork with two forks, then add as much of the cooking liquid as you'd like to saturate the pork.
4. While the pork cooks, make the salsa. In a large bowl, combine the avocados, salsa verde, salt, and lime juice. Mash with a fork or potato masher until smooth. Cover and chill until ready to use.
5. Serve the pork with warm corn tortillas, pickled red onions, shredded Oaxaca cheese, and the prepared salsa. Drizzle with Mexican crema. Store leftover pork in a sealed container in the fridge for up to 5 days.

PASTEL DE TRES LECHES

SERVINGS: 12 to 16 | **COOK TIME:** 45 minutes active, 30 minutes baking, 2 hours chilling
DIFFICULTY: Intermediate | **DIETARY:** Vegetarian

The name "three-milk cake" comes from the tasty soak applied in the recipe's final step. You start by whipping up and baking a moist vanilla sheet cake with a hint of orange zest. Once it cools, whisk together your three milks—condensed, evaporated, and whole—and pour slowly, a cupful at a time, over the cake. Cover and chill, and then finish with a topping of freshly whipped cream. Light and fresh, but with a rich flavor just extravagant enough to feel like you've hit the Starburst jackpot.

CAKE

2½ cups all-purpose flour

2½ teaspoons baking powder

1 teaspoon kosher salt

6 large eggs, separated

1½ cups granulated sugar

1 tablespoon vanilla extract

1 teaspoon orange zest

½ cup whole milk

TRES LECHES SOAK AND TOPPING

Two 14-ounce cans sweetened, condensed milk

One 12-ounce can evaporated milk

1½ cups whole milk

1½ cups heavy cream

¼ cup powdered sugar

1. Preheat the oven to 350°F. In a small bowl, sift together the flour, baking powder, and salt. Set aside.
2. In a large bowl (or bowl of a stand mixer fitted with the paddle attachment) with a handheld electric mixer on high, beat the egg yolks and ½ cup of sugar until thick and ribbony, 4 to 7 minutes. Beat in the vanilla and orange zest until smooth.
3. Add one-third of the flour mixture and mix in on low speed until just incorporated. Mix in half the milk, mixing until smooth. Repeat until you've used up the remaining flour mixture and milk, alternating between the two and ending with the last third of the flour mixture.
4. In a separate, clean bowl, using clean beaters (or the bowl of a stand mixer fitted with the whisk attachment), beat the egg yolks on medium speed until foamy, 2 to 3 minutes. Increase the speed to medium-high and continue beating while gradually adding the remaining 1 cup of sugar, until soft peaks form, 2 to 4 minutes longer.
5. Scoop out about one-quarter of the egg whites and stir by hand into the egg yolk mixture to loosen it up. Fold in the remaining egg whites until no streaks remain. Pour the batter into an ungreased 9-by-13-inch cake pan. Bake until golden brown on top and a toothpick inserted into the center of the cake comes out clean, 25 to 30 minutes.
6. Place the cake pan on a wire cooling rack and let cool for 1 hour. Poke all over with a fork. In a spouted pitcher or mixing bowl, whisk together the condensed milk, evaporated milk, and whole milk. Pour the mixture all over the cake about 1 cup at a time (totally okay to eyeball this), wait 5 minutes, then add the next cup. Cover the cake pan and chill in the fridge for 2 hours.
7. In a large bowl with an electric mixer on medium-high speed, beat together the heavy cream and powdered sugar until soft peaks form, 2 to 4 minutes. Spread all over the cake and serve. Leftover cake should be covered and chilled and will keep fresh for up to 3 days.

North Atlantic Operating
Company, Inc.

SAN FIERRO

So, let's review: Vice City is the beachfront where billion-dollar deals are sealed with rum runners and a Cuban cigar. Las Venturas is the desert where you have fun losing your money, dignity, and sometimes a couple of fingers. Liberty City is the global center of finance—fast-paced, densely vertical, angry. Los Santos is the global center of entertainment—a laid-back, horizontal sprawl of people writing screenplays. And then there's San Fierro, your global center of tech nerds in black T-shirts who currently rule the world.

The City by the Bay is famous for a lot of things: progressive dogma, Beat bookstores, Hashbury's "Summer of Love" tie-dye headbands. Sustainability, Save the Redwoods, Save the Whales, Save the BAWSAQ. For our purposes in this cookbook, San Fierro is also famous for its unique culinary scene—one that many experts rate as the best in America. It offers everything from its Chinatown dim sum to fresh-caught Dungeness crab and seafood cioppino to its world-famous sourdough bread and the Wharf's Fierro Fudge. Let's check out some star recipes from our Bay Area favorites.

PASTAGEDDON

With bustling locations in both the Hashbury and Garcia districts, Pastageddon is a longtime San Fierro tradition. This venerable mainstay of the Bay Area's culinary ecosystem is such a bright light, not even a voracious singularity could dim its glow. Whether you're a cop or a contract killer (or both), you can feel safe bringing your wife and kids to its unrivaled Italian-style family dining even though the menu proclaims, "Our wine list is longer than the Leone Family's police record!" That menu also features two of our favorite no-frills appetizer recipes: bread and meatballs.

ITALIAN JOB WHISKEY SOUR

SERVINGS: 1 | **COOK TIME:** 5 minutes | **DIFFICULTY:** Easy | **DIETARY:** Vegetarian, Gluten free

After you pull off a particularly spectacular heist, it's so much fun to ditch your Issi in the Bay then slam some ill-gotten loot on the bar for this, Pastageddon's signature cocktail. Better yet, shake it up yourself—your crew will be impressed. It's a fun riff on the classic sour, adding a shot of amaretto to the whiskey and freshly squeezed lemon juice. This concoction ticks all the basics of a good cocktail—sweet, sour, and spirit. Don't forget the standard bartender's double-shake technique: combine ingredients, shake once, then add ice and shake again.

1 ounce lemon juice

1 teaspoon Italian cocktail cherry juice

1½ ounces amaretto

1 ounce whiskey

½ ounce egg white (about ½ large egg white)

Orange slice

Cocktail cherry

1. In a cocktail shaker, combine the lemon juice, cocktail cherry juice, amaretto, and whiskey. Shake vigorously for 15 seconds, until foamy.
2. Fill the cocktail shaker with ice, close the shaker, and shake vigorously again until the outside of the shaker is frosty.
3. Strain into a rocks glass full of ice. Garnish with an orange slice and cocktail cherry. Serve immediately.

PARMESAN FOCACCIA

SERVINGS: 6 to 8 | **COOK TIME:** 15 minutes active, 24–96 hours chilling, 1 to 2 hours rising, 25 minutes baking
DIFFICULTY: Intermediate | **DIETARY:** Vegetarian

This flat baked bread, crunchy outside and soft as a pillow inside, requires a bit of time and patience in the prep—in particular, you want to mix the dough and chill it a day in advance, then let it rise an hour or two in the pan the next day. But when the dough's ready to bake, you get to (1) jab your fingers to "dimple the dough," which is always fun, and (2) smell the bread baking, which is only surpassed by (3) eating it on the rooftop garden of your safehouse at the crest of Windy, Windy, Windy, Windy Street.

4 cups bread flour

2 teaspoons kosher salt

6 tablespoons grated Parmesan, divided

1½ teaspoons active dry yeast

1⅔ cups lukewarm water

8 tablespoons olive oil, divided

1. In a large bowl, combine the flour, salt, 4 tablespoons of Parmesan, and the yeast. Stir, then add the water and 4 tablespoons of olive oil. Stir until well combined and no patches of dry flour remain. Cover the bowl and chill in the fridge for at least 24 hours, or up to 4 days.
2. Pour 2 tablespoons of oil into a 9-by-13-inch metal cake pan. Tilt the pan to coat all over with the oil, making sure the bottom and sides are well coated. Transfer the dough to the pan, pressing and stretching the dough into an even layer. Cover and let rise in a warm spot for 1 to 2 hours, until puffy, doubled in volume, and the dough completely fills the pan.
3. While the dough rises, preheat the oven to 450°F. Once the dough has risen, dampen your hands with warm water and quickly dimple the dough by slamming your fingertips (like vigorously playing the piano) into the dough all over, four or five times.
4. Drizzle the dough with the remaining 2 tablespoons of olive oil, and sprinkle with the remaining Parmesan. Bake for 20 to 25 minutes, until golden brown on top. Let cool in the pan for 5 minutes before transferring to a wire cooling rack to cool just enough to safely handle. Serve hot. Focaccia is best eaten on the day it's made, but leftovers should be tightly wrapped in plastic or foil and stored at room temperature for up to 1 day.

MARINA MEATBALLS

SERVINGS: 8 meatballs | **COOK TIME:** 1 hour 20 minutes | **DIFFICULTY:** Easy | **DIETARY:** N/A

Follow the breadcrumbs to Pastageddon's most celebrated starter dish. Feasting on these jumbo, oven-roasted beef and pork meatballs is like live-blogging a Bolingbroke jailbreak—the only sad moment is when it's all over. Chef Jimi H serves his Marina balls on a bed of homemade red sauce topped with Parmesan and a signature seasoning blend. Then, says Jimi, "We imbue it with a dash of Hashbury street-love." Whatever that is, it must be good. (Note: This dish pairs well with the Parmesan Focaccia [page 118] and a nice Chianti.)

FOR MEATBALLS

2 tablespoons olive oil

1 medium yellow or white onion, diced

1 large red bell pepper, diced

4 cloves garlic, minced

2 large eggs

¼ cup heavy cream

½ cup plain breadcrumbs

1 cup grated Parmesan, divided

1 pound ground beef

1 pound ground pork

2 teaspoons kosher salt

1 teaspoon dried oregano

1 teaspoon black pepper

½ teaspoon dried thyme

¼ teaspoon ground fennel

FOR SAUCE

2 tablespoons olive oil

1 small yellow or white onion, finely chopped

6 cloves garlic, minced

Pinch red pepper flakes

One 28-ounce can whole plum tomatoes

1 teaspoon kosher salt

½ teaspoon black pepper

1 large sprig basil

1. Preheat the oven to 400°F. Line a half-sheet pan with parchment paper.
2. In a large Dutch oven, heat the oil over medium-high heat until shimmering. Add the onion and bell pepper and cook, stirring occasionally, until softened and the onions are just beginning to brown at the edges, 7 to 10 minutes. Stir in the garlic and cook, stirring constantly, until fragrant, about 1 minute longer. Remove from the heat and transfer the contents to a large heatproof bowl.
3. While the onion mixture cools, in a small bowl, beat together the eggs and heavy cream. Stir in the breadcrumbs and ½ cup of Parmesan.
4. Crumble the ground beef and pork on the top of the onion mixture. Season all over with the salt, black pepper, oregano, and thyme, then add the egg mixture from step 3. Work the mixture with your hands until well combined.
5. Shape the meat mixture into eight large balls, then transfer to the prepared pan. Roast the meatballs until deeply browned all over, 25 to 35 minutes, turning the meatballs about halfway through the cooking process.
6. While the meatballs cook, prepare the sauce. In the same large Dutch oven you used in step 2, heat the oil over medium-high heat until shimmering, then add the onions. Cook, stirring occasionally, until softened and turning brown at the edges, 7 to 10 minutes. Add the garlic and cook, stirring constantly, until fragrant, 1 minute longer. Add the red pepper flakes, tomatoes, salt, pepper, and basil. Increase the heat and bring to a boil while mashing the tomatoes with a potato masher or the back of a wooden spoon, then reduce to a simmer.
7. Let the sauce simmer until the meatballs are done roasting, remove the basil, then add the meatballs to the sauce. Cover and continue simmering, stirring occasionally, until reduced and thickened, about 15 to 20 minutes longer.
8. To serve, spoon the sauce onto a serving platter, then top with the meatballs. Top each meatball with more sauce, then sprinkle the remaining Parmesan over them. Store leftover meatballs and sauce in a sealed container in the fridge for up to 5 days.

THE BEARDED CLAM SEAFOOD BISTRO

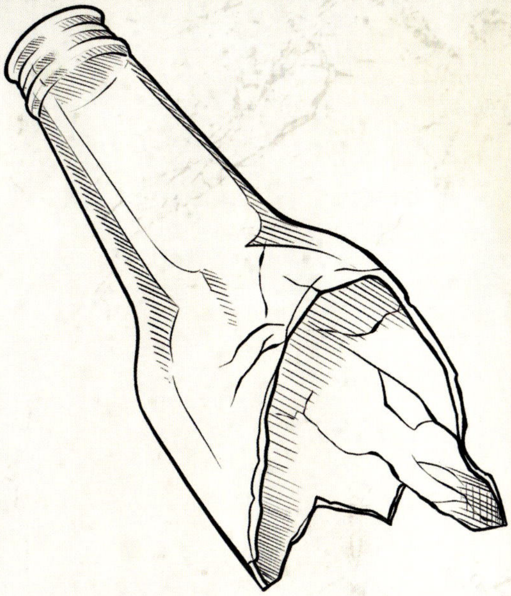

This upscale seafood restaurant with the refined tagline "We've got crabs!" is nestled in San Fierro's fabled Hashbury district, the longtime hippie capital of the Western world. It seems an odd fit, but the Hashbury location has proved so successful that ownership eventually expanded operations to the East Coast, opening three new Clams in Liberty City. Of course, the City by the Bay, so highly evolved in its culture-smug, naturally considers San Fierro's original to be the One True Clam. But the fact is, once you slide inside any Bearded Clam, you never want to leave. The seafood is fresh-caught and flawless, and the exquisite cold bar is typically packed with tech-world luminaries (and their coke suppliers) washing down Kumamoto oysters with Clammy Cocktails and Sierra Madre Mojitos (page 128).

SEARED SCALLOPS "LA VIE EN ROSE"

SERVINGS: 2 | **COOK TIME:** 40 minutes | **DIFFICULTY:** Intermediate | **DIETARY:** Gluten free

Life in San Fierro, seen in rosy hues, can be as beautiful as Édith Piaf's signature song. That's why the Clam's chef created this remarkably upbeat dish for lovers, then named it after the iconic tune. Delicate scallops seared to perfection, served with a savory raspberry rose sauce and a garnish of edible rose petals for that final, indescribable *je ne sais quoi*. Pair it with a glass of the 1982 Château Lafite Rothschild. Then top off the evening with a romantic tram ride up the hill to your Calton Heights flat.

SAVORY RASPBERRY ROSE SAUCE

2 tablespoons olive oil

1 small shallot, minced

1 clove garlic, minced

Salt

Pepper

1 cup rose wine

3 sprigs fresh thyme

6 ounces fresh raspberries

¼ cup heavy cream

2 tablespoons unsalted butter

Few drops rose water

SEARED SCALLOPS

12 ounces fresh sea scallops, patted dry with paper towels

½ teaspoon kosher salt

¼ teaspoon black pepper

2 tablespoons olive oil

Dried edible rose petals, for garnish

1. Make the savory raspberry sauce. In a medium skillet, heat the oil over medium-high heat until shimmering. Add the shallot and garlic, season with a good pinch of salt and pepper, and cook, stirring constantly, until fragrant and softened, about 2 minutes. Add the wine and thyme, bring to a boil and reduce, stirring occasionally, until reduced by about half, 2 to 4 minutes.
2. Stir in the raspberries and cook, stirring occasionally, until the raspberries break down completely, 4 to 6 minutes. Remove from the heat, then remove the thyme stems. Transfer to the bowl of a food processor or blender and pulse until smooth.
3. Pass the purée through a fine-mesh strainer into a small saucepan and discard any solids. Place over medium heat and bring up to a simmer. Stir in the heavy cream and cook until thickened enough to coat the back of a spoon, 3 to 5 minutes. Stir in the butter and rose water. Season to taste with additional salt and pepper if needed.
4. While working through step 3, cook the scallops. Season them all over with salt and pepper, then heat the oil in a large nonstick skillet over medium-high heat. Cook for 2 to 3 minutes on both sides until well seared and opaque all the way through. Ideally, the sauce and scallops should finish cooking at roughly the same time. Remove the scallops from the heat.
5. Spoon a few tablespoons of the sauce in a circular pool at the outer edge of two plates. Place a large spoon at the center of the pool and swipe along the outside edge of the plate to create a comet-shaped streak. Divide the scallops between both dishes, lining them up along the streak of sauce. Drizzle with a little more sauce, then scatter edible rose petals over the top. Serve immediately.

CLAMMY COCKTAIL

SERVINGS: 1 | **COOK TIME:** 5 minutes | **DIFFICULTY:** Easy | **DIETARY:** Gluten free

It may seem counterintuitive that anything clammy could sustain a great drink, but here it is—indisputable proof in the form of yet another bold San Fierro original. Vodka, tomato juice, and lime juice to start; add Worcestershire, hot sauce, and then splashes of clam juice and pickle brine; garnish with a celery stick and a lime wedge. If it seems like a Bloody Mary, you're right, it is. But you'll find that the clam juice brings out a delicious seafood/umami depth that you can't get from your classic Mary.

4 ounces tomato juice
2 ounces vodka
½ ounce clam juice
½ ounce lime juice
½ ounce pickle brine
2 dashes Worcestershire sauce
2 dashes vinegar-based hot sauce
Lime wedge
Celery salt
Celery stalk

1. In a cocktail shaker filled with ice, add the tomato juice, vodka, clam juice, lime juice, pickle brine, Worcestershire sauce, and hot sauce. Pour the contents of the shaker into an empty shaker or the other half of the shaker. Repeat four or five times.
2. Run the lime wedge around the rim of a tall glass. Dip in the celery salt to coat the rim, then fill the glass with ice. Strain the mixture from step 1 into the glass, then garnish with the celery stalk. Serve immediately.

SIERRA MADRE MOJITO

SERVINGS: 1 | **COOK TIME:** 3 minutes | **DIFFICULTY:** Easy | **DIETARY:** Vegan, Gluten free

This remarkably refreshing minty cocktail is named after the secluded mountainous region of San Andreas known as a hotbed of drug smuggling, human trafficking, and paramilitary training camps. Ironically, the Sierra Madre Mojito is the trendy favorite of all the former flower children and rainbow warriors who ended up stumbling into venture capital then funding tech-bro startups like Bleeter, Lifeinvader, and Fruit Computers. Everybody got rich, and so . . . mojitos all around!

6 mint leaves
1 lemon slice, halved
2 lime slices, divided
1 orange slice, halved
1 ounce simple syrup
½ ounce lime juice
2 ounces white rum
Club soda

1. In the bottom of a tall glass, muddle the mint, lemon slice, one lime slice, orange slice, simple syrup, and lime juice several times to release the juices from the citrus and oils from the mint.
2. Pour in the rum and stir well to combine. Fill the glass with ice, then top with club soda. Garnish with the remaining lime slice and serve immediately.

STREET EATS

Every great American city brings its very best foods right to the street. chili dog stands, taco and tamale trucks, ice-cream vans, pho pods, Jamaican jerk shacks, fish-and-chips kiosks—so many mouthwatering varieties of food, right there on the sidewalk, delighting pedestrian nostrils with mind-blowing aromas. We've even expanded our definition of street food to include a couple of favorite chains as well, because sometimes you're just hungry for the familiar and convenient when you're planning your next heist.

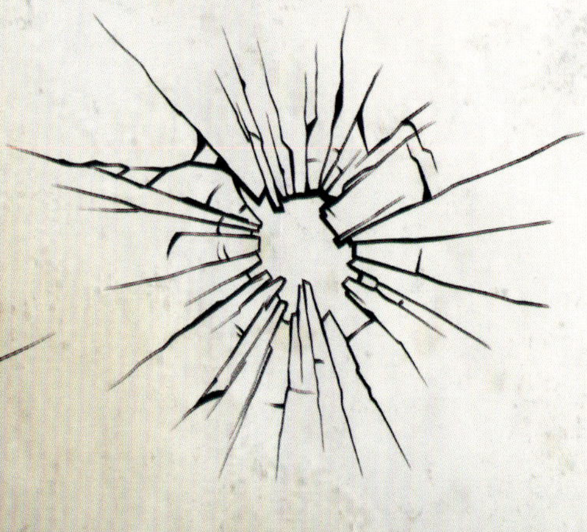

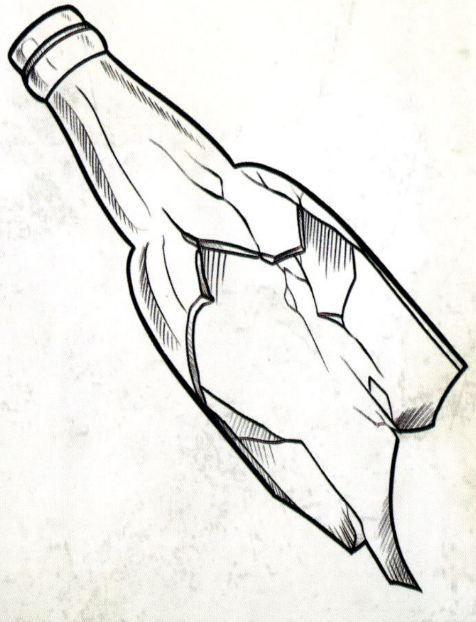

CHILI CHEESE DOG

SERVINGS: 4 | **COOK TIME:** 15 minutes | **DIFFICULTY:** Easy | **DIETARY:** N/A

East meets West in this Chili Dog rendering of the classic street dog. Start by whipping up a batch of San Fierro's special queso sauce, creamy and smooth. Then heat up a cup of Liberty City MC Chili, the finest in the land. (Check out the recipe in our Liberty City chapter.) Slap any decent hot dog on a bun and pour it all on. Street meat has never been such an exhilarating treat.

QUESO

⅓ cup whole milk

4 ounces American cheese, shredded (or cut into fine diced cubes)

4 ounces pepper jack cheese, shredded

Half 14-ounce can fire-roasted tomatoes with green chiles, well drained (see note)

Few dashes hot sauce (optional)

TO ASSEMBLE

1 tablespoon neutral oil, such as canola or safflower

4 hot dogs

4 hot dog buns, warmed (preferably split-top)

1 cup Liberty City MC Chili (page 37), hot

1. In a small saucepan, bring the milk to a simmer over medium heat. Whisking constantly, add both cheeses, a small pinch at a time, until all of it has been incorporated and the sauce is smooth and creamy.
2. Stir in the diced tomatoes and chiles, along with the hot sauce, if using. Keep the queso over very low heat, stirring occasionally, until ready to use.
3. In a small skillet, heat the oil over medium heat until shimmering. Add the hot dogs and sear, flipping occasionally, until browned all over and warmed through, 5 to 7 minutes.
4. Transfer the hot dogs to the warmed buns, then divide among four plates. Top each hot dog with about ¼ cup of chili and a good drizzle of queso. Store leftover queso in a sealed container in the fridge for up to 5 days. To reheat, return to a saucepan and heat gently over low to medium-low heat, stirring constantly, until creamy and liquid—if needed, add a splash of milk to thin it out.

SPRUNK!

SERVINGS: 1 unit of SPRUNK! | **COOK TIME:** 40 minutes, plus cooling time | **DIFFICULTY:** Easy | **DIETARY:** Vegan, Gluten free

Crime kingpins don't have much in common with the regular Joe on the street, or with their own syndicate soldiers, for that matter. But there's one powerful bond that crosses every level of stratification in America, every boundary of class: Everybody loves Sprunk! After all, it's "The Essence of Life!" For years, the monolithic manufacturer of Sprunk kept its secret formula under tight wraps. Now, at the risk of corporate reprisal with extreme prejudice, we unveil that Sprunk recipe. Or, at least, one Sprunk recipe. Please contact the Sprunk Company if you have any legal questions.

LEMON-LIME SYRUP

Juice and zest of 4 limes

Juice and zest of 4 lemons

1 cup sugar

TO SERVE

12 ounces seltzer

1. In a small saucepan, combine the lime and lemon juices and zests and sugar. Heat over medium-low, stirring constantly, until the sugar dissolves. Remove from the heat, cover, and let steep for 30 minutes. Strain into a heatproof bowl, let cool to room temperature, then transfer to a sealed container (a swingtop glass bottle works great for this). The syrup will keep in the fridge for up to 1 week.
2. When ready to serve, pour 1 to 2 tablespoons of syrup into a tall glass filled with ice. Pour over the seltzer and gently stir to combine. Serve immediately.

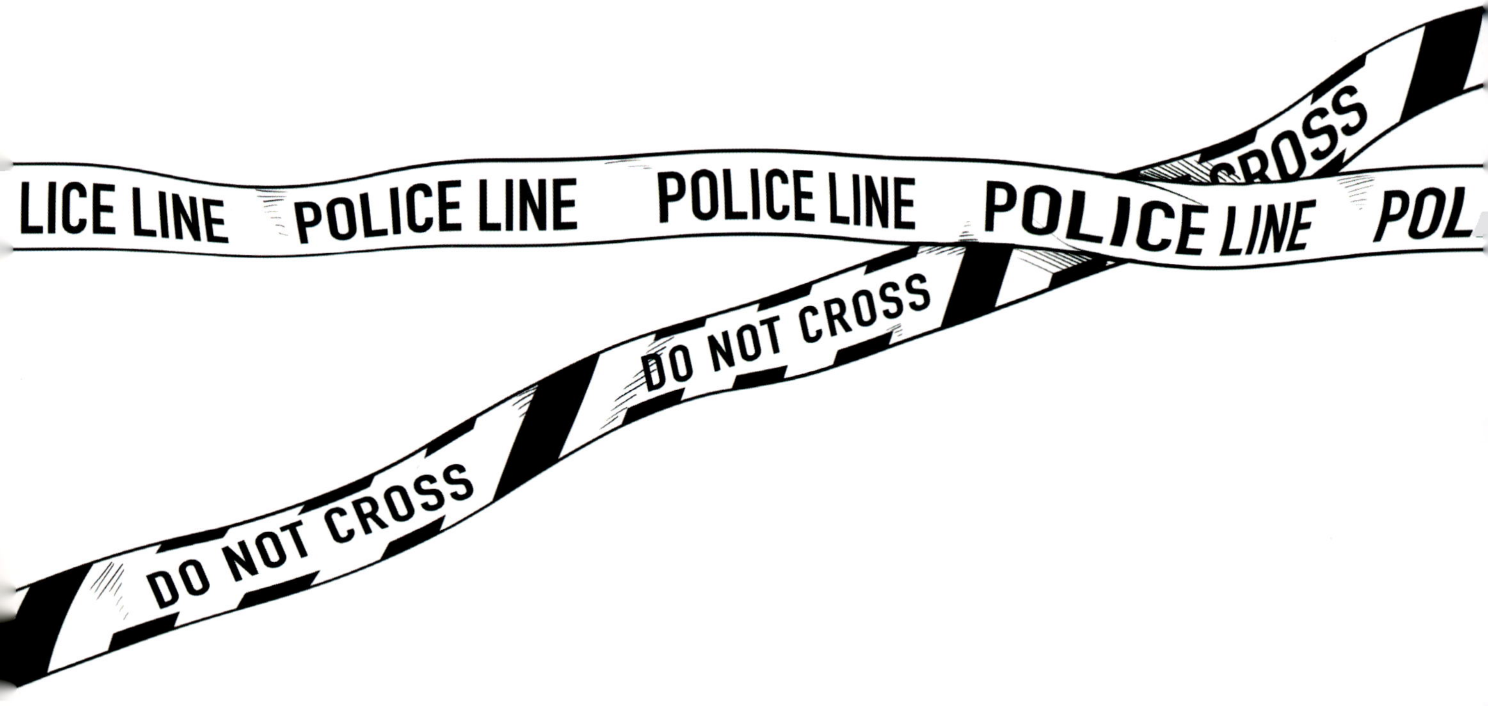

PIG & PEPPERS PIE

SERVINGS: 6 to 8 | **COOK TIME:** 3 hours (up to 4 days) | **DIFFICULTY:** Intermediate | **DIETARY:** N/A

The Well Stacked Pizza Co. is the most venerable name in America's burgeoning well stacked pizza industry. Nobody would argue that anybody stacks pizza quite as well as Well Stacked does, and this particular recipe is a perfect example of that corporate ethos: sweet Italian sausage and roasted red bell peppers piled high on a crust rolled from slowly fermented dough then ladled with a thick homemade sauce based on luscious peeled plum tomatoes. Must we write more? No, so let's end with the classic franchise slogan: *"You want a pizza or what?"*

DOUGH

½ cup fine semolina

2 teaspoons active dry yeast

1½ cups lukewarm water

3½ cups 00 flour

1 tablespoon kosher salt

7 tablespoons olive oil, divided

PIZZA SAUCE

One 28-ounce can peeled plum tomatoes

2 teaspoons oregano

2 teaspoons kosher salt

1½ teaspoons granulated sugar

1 pinch red pepper flakes

TO ASSEMBLE

12 ounces shredded mozzarella cheese

1 cup pizza sauce

2 tablespoons olive oil

2 sweet Italian sausages, casings removed

2 roasted red bell peppers, drained and sliced into 1-inch-long strips

TO MAKE THE DOUGH

1. In the bowl of a stand mixer, whisk the semolina, yeast, and water, then let sit for 5 minutes, until bubbling. Add the flour, salt, and 3 tablespoons of olive oil. Mix with the dough hook attachment on low speed until a shaggy dough forms. Increase the speed to medium and let knead until smooth and elastic (about 15 minutes).
2. From here, you can proceed directly to baking. However, pizza dough tastes best when it's allowed to slowly ferment in the fridge. Place in a lightly oiled 6-quart sealable container and keep in the fridge for 24 hours or up to 4 days. If you go this route, remove from the fridge and let come to room temperature for 1 hour before proceeding to the next step. Otherwise, skip this process entirely.
3. Pour the remaining 4 tablespoons of oil into a clean half-sheet pan. Rub all over, including the inner sides of the pan. Add the dough to the pan, flip to coat in the oil, then stretch the dough into a rectangle. Cover with plastic wrap or, if you have a spare half-sheet pan, invert the pan and set it on top so the edges are lined up. Let sit for 1½ to 2 hours until well puffed.

TO MAKE THE PIZZA SAUCE

4. While the dough is rising, make the sauce. In the bowl of a food processor, pulse the tomatoes, oregano, 2 teaspoons of salt, 1½ teaspoons of granulated sugar, and red pepper flakes until the mixture is mostly smooth with some very small chunks of tomato (lentil-size chunks at the largest) remaining. Transfer the sauce to an airtight container and store in the refrigerator until you're ready to use it. Sauce may be prepared up to 5 days in advance.

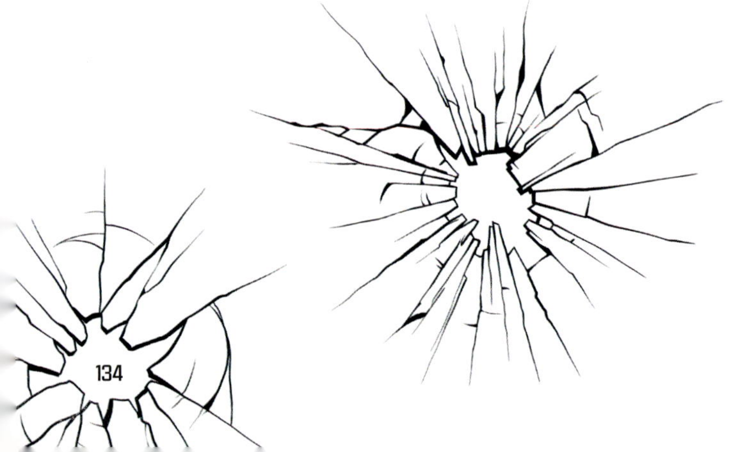

TO ASSEMBLE AND BAKE

5. Toward the end of the rising time, place an oven rack on the lower third position. Preheat the oven to 550°F.
6. Precook the sausage while the dough rises and the oven preheats. Heat 2 tablespoons olive oil in a large skillet over medium-high heat until shimmering. Add the sausage and cook, breaking apart into small chunks with a wooden spoon, until cooked through, 5 to 8 minutes. Drain the excess oil, and set aside.
7. When the dough has risen, gently stretch the dough to fill the pan. It will deflate slightly, but that's okay—just be careful not to completely flatten the dough as you work. Spread the pizza sauce over the dough, then top with the mozzarella cheese, followed by the sausage and bell peppers.
8. Bake the pizza for 10 to 12 minutes, until the cheese is golden and the bottom of the crust is a deep golden brown. Cut into squares, and serve.

   NOTE: Feel free to replace the homemade pizza sauce with your favorite store-bought sauce.

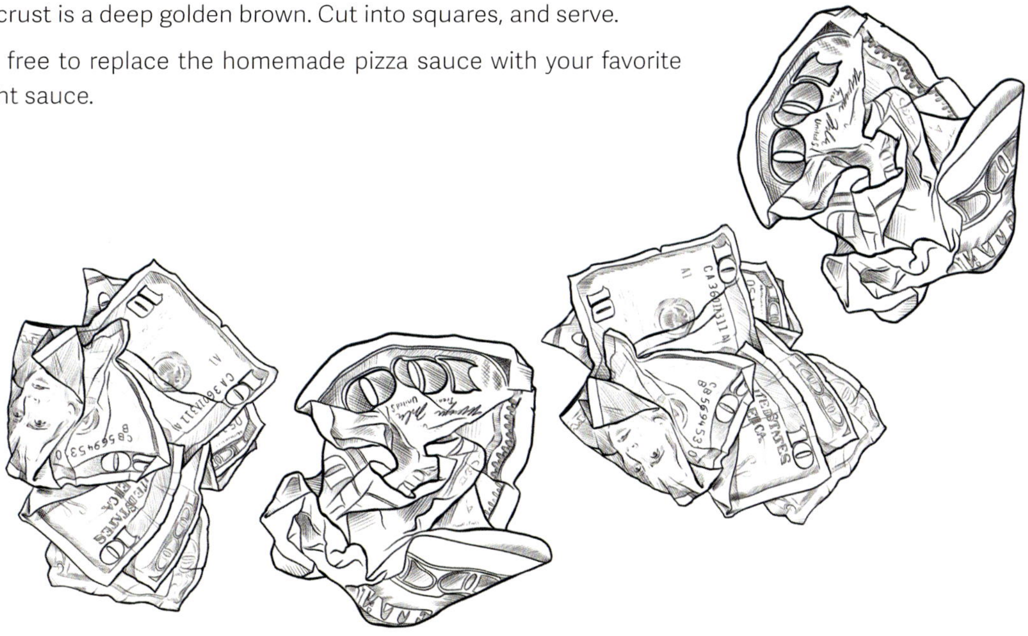

CLUCKIN' BELL CHICKEN FINGERS AND FRIES

SERVINGS: 4 | **COOK TIME:** 1 hour 15 minutes, plus 1 hour marinating | **DIFFICULTY:** Intermediate | **DIETARY:** N/A

Who says fast food has to be greasy, unhealthy, and disgusting? Okay, nobody says that . . . but insipid fast food does seem like a verity of modern life. That's why at Cluckin' Bell, things are different. The Bell's zesty fingers & fries require a bit of careful timing to prepare at home, but the payoff is like a bag of unmarked $100 bills. The recipe's pickle brine marinade takes your chicken tenders to the best end of the savory spectrum, and the vinegar-kissed fries may induce the same kind of psychoactive euphoria typically peddled by Vespucci Beach vendors. Enjoy!

TENDERS

1 pound chicken tenders

½ cup pickle brine

½ cup buttermilk

1 large egg

1 tablespoon vinegar-based hot sauce

1 cup all-purpose flour

¼ cup cornstarch

1 tablespoon kosher salt

1 tablespoon black pepper

1 tablespoon onion powder

1 teaspoon garlic powder

1½ quarts neutral oil

FRIES

2 pounds russet potatoes, peeled

1 tablespoon white vinegar

2½ tablespoons kosher salt, divided

2 quarts neutral oil

TO SERVE

Ranch dressing

Blue cheese dressing

Hot sauce

Ketchup

1. Place the chicken tenders in a sealable container or plastic bag, along with the pickle brine. Seal and chill for at least 1 hour or up to 12 hours.
2. Fill a large bowl with cold water. Cut the potatoes to ¼-by-¼-inch batons. As you work, place the cut potatoes into the cold water to soak.
3. Drain the potatoes and place into a large pot. Cover with fresh cold water, along with the vinegar and 2 tablespoons of kosher salt. Bring to a boil over high heat. Once the water begins boiling, set a timer for 10 minutes. Check the potatoes—they should be completely tender, but hold their shape.
4. While the potatoes cook, line a half-sheet pan with paper towels. Drain the potatoes and lay them on the paper towel-lined pan. Let cool while you heat the oil.
5. Add 2 quarts neutral oil to a large Dutch oven. Bring to 400°F over medium-high heat. Line a second half-sheet pan with paper towels. Add about one-third of the fries to the hot oil and cook for about 1 minute while stirring constantly with a slotted spoon or wire mesh spider strainer.
6. Transfer the fries to the second prepared sheet pan. Repeat with half the remaining fries, cooking and stirring for 1 minute before transferring to the prepared sheet pan. Finally, repeat with the remaining fries. Let the fries cool for 30 minutes at room temperature. Leave the fry oil in the Dutch oven, but keep it off heat.
7. While the fries cool, prepare the chicken tenders. Drain them of the pickle brine completely and pat dry with paper towels.
8. Whisk the buttermilk, egg, and hot sauce together in a wide, shallow bowl. Whisk the flour, cornstarch, salt, pepper, onion powder, and garlic powder together in a separate wide, shallow bowl.
9. Pour the oil into a large cast-iron skillet. It should reach a depth of about 2 inches. Heat the oil to 325°F to 340°F over medium heat.
10. While the oil heats, dip the tenders, one at a time, in the buttermilk mixture. Let the excess drip off, then dredge in the flour mixture. Shake off the excess, then transfer to a clean plate. Heat oven to 200°F and place a wire cooling rack into a half-sheet pan.

11. Add half the tenders to the hot oil and cook, turning every 1 to 2 minutes, until golden and cooked through, 4 to 6 minutes. Transfer to the wire cooling rack set in the sheet pan and keep warm in the oven. Repeat with the remaining tenders.
12. While the remaining tenders cook, bring the french fry oil back up to 400°F. Fry half of the fries for 3 to 4 minutes, until golden and crisp. Transfer to a metal mixing bowl lined with paper towels and season with kosher salt to taste. Transfer these fries to the wire cooling rack set in the sheet pan in the oven to keep warm.
13. Repeat step 12 with the remaining fries. Divide the tenders and fries between four plates and serve with your desired sauces.

NEW CHEESY STEAKOUT SUB

SERVINGS: 4 subs | **COOK TIME:** 20 minutes | **DIFFICULTY:** Easy | **DIETARY:** N/A

Shaved steak is one of America's greatest industrial innovations, matched only by the timeless brilliance of melted American cheese slices. Layer these on a warmed roll then add thinly sliced onion, chopped mushrooms, and shimmering strips of skillet-fried red bell peppers. Lastly, season with salt, pepper, and a dash of oregano. What you've created is an item listed in the National Registry of Iconic Foods . . . and a coast-to-coast favorite of FIB goons, mobsters, and every permutation in-between.

- 2 large red bell peppers, stems and seeds removed
- 2 tablespoons olive oil
- 1 small onion, thinly sliced
- 8 ounces mushrooms, coarsely chopped
- 24 ounces shaved steak
- Kosher salt
- Black pepper
- ½ teaspoon dried oregano
- Four 8-inch sub rolls, warmed
- 8 slices American cheese

1. Cut the bell peppers into strips that are about 1 inch long and ¼ inch wide. Heat the oil in a large skillet over medium-high heat until shimmering, then add the peppers, onions, and mushrooms. Season with ½ teaspoon each kosher salt and black pepper. Cook, stirring occasionally, until the onions are translucent and just beginning to turn brown at the edges, 8 to 12 minutes.
2. Add the shaved steak and cook, while tearing the meat into bits with two wooden spoons or spatulas, until cooked through. Season with 1 teaspoon each of kosher salt and black pepper, along with ½ teaspoon dried oregano.
3. Divide the meat, peppers, onions, and mushrooms between the four sub rolls and immediately top with two slices of American cheese each. Allow the cheese to melt for about 1 minute, then serve.

THE CUBANO MISSILE CRISIS

SERVINGS: 4 subs | **COOK TIME:** 4 hours 20 minutes | **DIFFICULTY:** Intermediate | **DIETARY:** N/A

In 1962, JFK stared down Nikita Khrushchev over the placement of Soviet ballistic missiles in Cuba just 90 miles from America's southern shore. For thirteen days, the world teetered on the brink of an apocalyptic nuclear exchange. In the Cuban expatriate cafés of Vice City, that faceoff inspired a legendary delicacy. As Chef Santiago so eloquently put it: "Eat slow-roasted boneless pork shoulder sandwiches today, for tomorrow we die!" Fortunately, smart diplomacy de-escalated the potential Armageddon. Better yet, the Cubano lives on!

SLOW ROASTED PORK

2 pounds boneless pork shoulder cut to 2-inch chunks

⅓ cup pineapple juice

⅓ cup orange juice

¼ cup lime juice

1 tablespoon kosher salt

1 teaspoon black pepper

1½ teaspoons ground coriander

1 teaspoon ground cumin

1 teaspoon dried Mexican oregano (or marjoram)

1 small onion, sliced

3 cloves garlic, peeled and smashed

1 bay leaf

TO ASSEMBLE

4 Cuban rolls (or French rolls or sub rolls)

4 tablespoons unsalted butter, softened

Yellow mustard

8 slices Swiss cheese

8 slices deli ham

Cornichon pickles, halved lengthwise

1. Heat the oven to 275°F. Place the pork in a small Dutch oven or 8-by-8-inch baking dish, along with the pineapple juice, orange juice, lime juice, salt, pepper, coriander, cumin, Mexican oregano, onions, garlic, and bay leaf. Toss to combine, then cover and roast for 4 hours, until you can easily shred the meat with a fork. Discard the bay leaf. This can be done up to 5 days in advance—keep the pork in a sealed container in the fridge until ready to use.
2. Gently warm the pork in a medium saucepan over medium heat, breaking apart and shredding with a wooden spoon until warmed through.
3. Halve the rolls lengthwise and spread the butter on the outside of the rolls (do not spread the butter on the cut sides). Spread yellow mustard on both of the cut sides of the rolls. Add one slice of Swiss cheese to each side of each roll, along with one slice of ham per roll, and as many sliced cornichons as you like.
4. Use a slotted spoon to drain the excess cooking liquid from the pork, and divide it between the rolls (you may have more pork than you need). Press the two halves of the rolls together to form the sandwiches.
5. Heat a panini press or place a large griddle or skillet over medium heat. Place the sandwiches in the press (you may need to do this in batches) and compress, cooking for 4 to 5 minutes, until crisp and golden brown and the cheese is melted. If using a griddle or skillet, place the sandwiches on the cooking surface, then compress them down with a large, flat metal spatula, or an additional heavy skillet. Cook for 4 to 5 minutes until golden brown, then flip and cook, pressing down with the spatula or skillet, for 4 to 5 minutes longer.
6. Cut the sandwiches in half diagonally, and serve hot.

CHERRY POPPERS CHOCOLATE CHUNK ICE CREA

SERVINGS: About 1 quart | **COOK TIME:** 20 minutes active, 8 hours chilling, plus churning | **DIFFICULTY:** Intermediate
DIETARY: Vegetarian, Gluten free

It's not easy to find commercial shills you can trust, but nobody cuts a more believable figure than Whoopee the Clown, right? The mascot of the Cherry Popper Ice Cream Company is beloved by dozens, perhaps even hundreds, coast to coast. You can find the Cherry Poppers brand in street stands and mobile vans and convenience stores throughout the Bay Area. And its cherry-chocolate chunk ice cream is a world-renowned San Fierro treat. The marketing tagline says it all: Cherry Poppers: "You'll Always Remember Your First!"

1 pound frozen cherries

1½ cups granulated sugar, divided

3 tablespoons cornstarch

½ teaspoon kosher salt

2½ cups half-and-half

2 teaspoons vanilla extract

1½ cups dark chocolate chunks (or coarsely chopped dark chocolate)

1. In a medium saucepan, combine the frozen cherries and 1 cup of sugar. Place over medium heat and cook, stirring occasionally, until the cherries release their juices and start to break down, 10 to 15 minutes.
2. Strain the cherry juice into a heatproof bowl through a colander or fine-mesh strainer. Reserve the cherries in a small bowl, covering and chilling them. Measure out 1 cup of the cherry juice and set aside. You can discard the rest or use it for another purpose.
3. In a medium saucepan or saucier, whisk together the remaining ½ cup of sugar, the cornstarch, and salt, making sure to break up any lumps of cornstarch. Whisk in the half-and-half in a steady stream, whisking until smooth. Whisk in the cherry juice. Place over medium heat and gently cook, whisking constantly, until the mixture starts to bubble. Once it does, set a timer for 1 minute and keep whisking vigorously until the timer goes off. Remove from the heat.
4. Strain the mixture into a heatproof bowl through a fine-mesh strainer, discarding any solids. Stir in the vanilla, cover, and chill for at least 4 hours or up to 5 days.
5. Drain the reserved cherries of any excess liquid and roughly chop them on a cutting board. Churn the ice-cream base according to your ice-cream machine's instructions. A few minutes before the ice cream is done churning, add the chopped cherries and chocolate chunks, letting the machine churn them until they're fully incorporated.
6. Transfer the ice cream to a quart-size freezer-safe container, seal, and freeze for at least 4 hours.

MEASUREMENT CONVERSIONS

VOLUME

U.S.	METRIC
⅕ teaspoon (tsp)	1 ml
1 teaspoon (tsp)	5 ml
1 tablespoon (tbsp)	15 ml
1 fluid ounce (fl. oz.)	30 ml
⅕ cup	50 ml
¼ cup	60 ml
⅓ cup	80 ml
3.4 fluid ounces	100 ml
½ cup	120 ml
⅔ cup	160 ml
¾ cup	180 ml
1 cup	240 ml
1 pint (2 cups)	480 ml
1 quart (4 cups)	.95 liter

WEIGHT

U.S.	METRIC
0.5 ounce (oz.)	14 grams
1 ounce (oz.)	28 grams
¼ pound (lb.)	113 grams
⅓ pound (lb.)	151 grams
½ pound (lb.)	227 grams
1 pound (lb.)	454 grams

TEMPERATURES

FAHRENHEIT	CELSIUS
200°	93°
212°	100°
250°	120°
275°	135°
300°	150°
325°	165°
350°	177°
400°	205°
425°	220°
450°	233°
475°	245°
500°	260°

ABOUT THE AUTHOR

Jarrett Melendez is a GLAAD Media Award- and Eisner Award-nominated comic and graphic novel writer, cookbook author, and food journalist. He's best known for the award-winning graphic novel *Chef's Kiss*, a queer romance set in a restaurant, which he co-created with Danica Brine. The sequel, *Chef's Kiss Again*, will be released in 2026. Jarrett has also contributed to award-winning and nominated anthologies, including *Young Men in Love*, *All We Ever Wanted*, and *Young Men in Love 2: New Romances*. Jarrett is currently working on *Tales of the Fungo: The Legend of Cep*, to be published by Andrews McMeel, *Fujoshi Warriors*, an action comedy graphic novel, and love letter to both fujoshis and magical girl anime and manga, and an upcoming licensed Webtoon.

As a cookbook author and food journalist, Jarrett has written countless articles and developed hundreds of original recipes that have appeared on Bon Appetit, Epicurious, Saveur and Food52. He's written numerous cookbooks, including *My Pokémon Baking Book*, *RuneScape: The Official Cookbook*, *Percy Jackson and the Olympians: The Official Cookbook*, *The Official Wednesday Cookbook*, *The Official Borderlands Cookbook*, *Persona: The Official Cookbook*, and *The White Lotus Official Cookbook*.

Jarrett grew up on the mean, deer-infested streets of Bucksport, Maine, but currently resides in Watertown, Massachusetts, with his partner Theo and a collection of Monokuro Boo plush pigs.

Jarrett would like to thank the lovely staff at Savenor's Butchery for their help procuring meat for developing these recipes (and for being an all around swell group of folks), Ray from Christina's Spice & Specialty Foods for always having the best spices in stock, Emily for taste testing and feedback, and his beloved Theo, for taste testing, supporting, and doing everything else they do.

Published by Titan Books, London, in 2025.

TITAN
BOOKS

A division of Titan Publishing Group Ltd
144 Southwark Street
London SE1 0UP
www.titanbooks.com

Find us on Facebook: www.facebook.com/TitanBooks
Follow us on X: @titanbooks

INSIGHT
EDITIONS

Published by arrangement with Insight Editions, San Rafael, California, in 2025. www.insighteditions.com

A CIP catalogue record for this title is available from the British Library.

EU RP (for authorities only)
eucomply OÜ Pärnu mnt 139b-14 11317
Talinn, Estonia
hello@eucompliancepartner.com
+3375690241

ISBN: 9781835416235

Publisher: Raoul Goff
SVP, Group Publisher: Vanessa Lopez
VP, Manufacturing: Alix Nicholaeff
Publishing Director: Mike Degler
Editorial Director: Jennifer Sims
Art Director: Catherine San Juan
Junior Designer: Samuel Louie
Managing Editor: Nora Milman
Production Manager: Deena Hashem
Strategic Production Planner: Lina s Palma-Temena

Illustrations by Chui Kanela

Photography by Waterbury Publications, Inc
Food Styling by Josh Hake

Manufactured in China by Insight Editions

10 9 8 7 6 5 4 3 2 1

ROOTS of PEACE REPLANTED PAPER

Insight Editions, in association with Roots of Peace, will plant two trees for each tree used in the manufacturing of this book. Roots of Peace is an internationally renowned humanitarian organization dedicated to eradicating land mines worldwide and converting war-torn lands into productive farms and wildlife habitats. Roots of Peace will plant two million fruit and nut trees in Afghanistan and provide farmers there with the skills and support necessary for sustainable land use.